First World War
and Army of Occupation
War Diary
France, Belgium and Germany

41 DIVISION
122 Infantry Brigade
Headquarters
1 July 1917 - 31 July 1917

WO95/2633/1

The Naval & Military Press Ltd
www.nmarchive.com
Published in association with The National Archives

Published by

The Naval & Military Press Ltd

Unit 10 Ridgewood Industrial Park,

Uckfield, East Sussex,

TN22 5QE England

Tel: +44 (0) 1825 749494

www.naval-military-press.com

www.nmarchive.com

This diary has been reprinted in facsimile from the original. Any imperfections are inevitably reproduced and the quality may fall short of modern type and cartographic standards.

© Crown Copyright
Images reproduced by permission of The National Archives, London, England, 2015.

Contents

Document type	Place/Title	Date From	Date To
Heading	WO95/2633/1		
Heading	Headquarters 122nd Inf. Bde. (41st Div) October 1917		
Miscellaneous	Cover for Documents. Nature of Enclosures.		
Miscellaneous	Headquarters, 41st Division. (A).	07/11/1917	07/11/1917
War Diary	La Panne.	01/10/1917	15/10/1917
War Diary	Coxyde Bains	16/10/1917	29/10/1917
War Diary	Synthe Area.	30/10/1917	31/10/1917
Operation(al) Order(s)	122nd Infantry Brigade Warning Order No. 12.	04/10/1917	04/10/1917
Miscellaneous	Administrative Instructions Reference 122nd Infantry Brigade Warning Order No. 12.	05/10/1917	05/10/1917
Miscellaneous	Location Of Units 41st Division.		
Operation(al) Order(s)	122nd Infantry Brigade Order No. 147.	05/10/1917	05/10/1917
Miscellaneous	March Table "A"		
Miscellaneous	Amendment To 122nd. Infantry Brigade Order No. 147.	06/10/1917	06/10/1917
Operation(al) Order(s)	122nd Infantry Brigade Warning Order No. 13	11/10/1917	11/10/1917
Miscellaneous	122nd Infantry Brigade Warning Order No. 13	11/10/1917	11/10/1917
Operation(al) Order(s)	122nd Infantry Brigade Order No. 148	12/10/1917	12/10/1917
Miscellaneous	March Table To Accompany 122nd Infantry Brigade Order No. 148.		
Miscellaneous	12th East Surrey Regt. 15th Hampshire Regt.	13/10/1917	13/10/1917
Operation(al) Order(s)	122nd Infantry Brigade Warning Order No. 14	25/10/1917	25/10/1917
Miscellaneous	122nd Infantry Brigade Warning Order. No. 15.	28/10/1917	28/10/1917
Operation(al) Order(s)	122nd Infantry Brigade Order No. 149	28/10/1917	28/10/1917
Miscellaneous	March Table To Accompany 122nd Infantry Brigade Order No. 149.		
Miscellaneous	122nd Infantry Brigade Coast Defence Scheme. Coxyde Bains Sector	23/10/1917	23/10/1917
Miscellaneous	122nd Infantry Brigade Coast Defence Scheme Coxyde Bains Sector. Appendix 'A'		
Miscellaneous	122nd Infantry Brigade Coast Defence Scheme Coxyde Bains Sector. Appendix 'B'		
Heading	122 Infy B.H.Q September 1917		
Miscellaneous			
Miscellaneous	On His Majesty's Service. O To A O C Section 3rd Echelon		
Miscellaneous	Headquarters, 41st Division. (A).	07/10/1917	07/10/1917
War Diary	Boisdingham	01/09/1917	17/09/1917
War Diary	Hedge St Tunnels.	17/09/1917	24/09/1917
War Diary	Caestre.	25/09/1917	27/09/1917
War Diary	La Panne.	28/09/1917	05/10/1917
Operation(al) Order(s)	Operation Orders No. 85 By Lieut Col. A. C. Corfe, D.S.O. Commanding 11th Bn. "The Queen's Own" Royal West Kent Regt. (Lewisham)	03/09/1917	03/09/1917
Operation(al) Order(s)	Operation Orders No. 86 By Lieut Col. A. C. Corfe, D.S.O. Commanding 11th Bn. "The Queen's Own" Royal West Kent Regt. (Lewisham)	09/09/1918	09/09/1918
Miscellaneous	Instructions To Accompany Operation Order No. 86 For Practice Attack	10/09/1917	10/09/1917

Operation(al) Order(s)	Operation Orders No. 87 By Lieut, Col. A. C. Corfe D.S.O. Commanding 11th Bn. "The Queen's Own" Royal West Kent Regt. (Lewisham)	11/09/1917	11/09/1917
Miscellaneous	Administrative Orders No. 1 Reference O.C. 87.		
Miscellaneous	Miscellaneous Instructions Reference O.C. 87		
Miscellaneous	Amendment To Operation Order 87.		
Diagram etc			
Miscellaneous	Administrative Orders No. 2. Reference O.O. 87.		
Miscellaneous	Instructions Reference O.O 87 And Miscellaneous Instructions To O.O. 87	11/09/1917	11/09/1917
Operation(al) Order(s)	Operation Orders No. 88 by Lieut. Col. A.C. Corfe. D.S.O. Commanding 11th Bn "The Queen's Own" Royal West Kent Regt. (Lewisham)	13/09/1917	13/09/1917
Miscellaneous	Code Of Signals For Offensive Operations Only.		
Operation(al) Order(s)	Operation Orders No. 88a. By Lieut Col. A. C. Corfe. D.S.O.commanding 11th Bn. "The Queen's Own" Royal West Kent Regt. (Lewisham).	15/09/1917	15/09/1917
Operation(al) Order(s)	Operation Orders No. 89. by Lieut Col. A. C. Corfe. D.S.O. Commanding 11th Bn. "The Queen's Own" Royal West Kent Regt. (Lewisham).	17/09/1917	17/09/1917
Operation(al) Order(s)	18th Bn. King's Royal Rifle Corps. Operation Order No. 139.	16/09/1917	16/09/1917
Miscellaneous			
Operation(al) Order(s)	18th Bn Rifle Operation Order No 139	23/09/1917	23/09/1917
Operation(al) Order(s)	18th Bn King's Royal Rifle Corps. Operation Order No 141.	26/09/1917	26/09/1917
Heading	HQ 122 Infy Batt (41st Div) Vol 16 August 1917		
Miscellaneous	On His Majesty's Service.		
Miscellaneous	Headquarters, 41st Division (A)	01/09/1917	01/09/1917
War Diary	Spoil Bank	01/08/1917	14/08/1917
War Diary	Elzenwalle	14/08/1917	14/08/1917
War Diary	La Rouklo-Shille	15/08/1917	19/08/1917
War Diary	Nieppe.	20/08/1917	20/08/1917
War Diary	Boisdingham	21/08/1917	31/08/1917
Map			
Miscellaneous	Message Pad.	05/08/1917	05/08/1917
Miscellaneous	Verbal Telephone Messages	05/08/1917	05/08/1917
Operation(al) Order(s)	122nd Infantry Brigade Order No. 130	05/08/1917	05/08/1917
Miscellaneous	122nd Infantry Brigade Intelligence Summary	06/08/1917	06/08/1917
Miscellaneous	Report On Operation Of July 31st 1917 & Subsequent Days.	06/09/1917	06/09/1917
Miscellaneous	Report On The Operations Which Took Place On The Morning Of The 5th August.	08/08/1917	08/08/1917
Operation(al) Order(s)	122nd Infantry Brigade Order No. 131.	08/08/1917	08/08/1917
Miscellaneous	Officer Commanding 15th Hampshire Regt. To: Headquarters, 122nd Infantry Brigade.	10/08/1917	10/08/1917
Operation(al) Order(s)	122nd Infantry Brigade Order No. 132	12/08/1917	12/08/1917
Miscellaneous	March Table To Accompany 122nd Infantry Brigade Order No. 132		
Miscellaneous	Reference 122nd Infantry Brigade Order No. 132	12/08/1917	12/08/1917
Operation(al) Order(s)	122nd Infantry Brigade Order No. 133	12/08/1917	12/08/1917
Miscellaneous	Amendment To 122nd Infantry Brigade Order No. 132.	12/08/1917	12/08/1917
Map			
Miscellaneous			
Operation(al) Order(s)	122nd Infantry Brigade Order No. 134	13/08/1917	13/08/1917
Miscellaneous	March and Embussing Table		

Miscellaneous	12th East Surrey Regt.	16/08/1917	16/08/1917
Miscellaneous	March Table		
Miscellaneous	12th East Surrey Regt. 15th Hampshire Regt.	16/08/1917	16/08/1917
Miscellaneous	March Table		
Miscellaneous	12th East Surrey Regt. 15th Hampshire Regt.	16/08/1917	16/08/1917
Miscellaneous	March Table		
Miscellaneous	122nd Infantry Brigade.	18/08/1917	18/08/1917
Miscellaneous	A Form. Messages And Signals.	19/08/1917	19/08/1917
Miscellaneous	Addendum to 122nd Infantry Brigade Order No. 135.	19/08/1917	19/08/1917
Operation(al) Order(s)	122nd Infantry Brigade Order No. 135.	19/08/1917	19/08/1917
Miscellaneous	March Table To Accompany 122nd Infantry Brigade Order No. 135		
Operation(al) Order(s)	122nd Infantry Brigade Order No 136.	20/08/1917	20/08/1917
Miscellaneous	March Table		
Miscellaneous	Bus Table		
Heading	Headquarters 122nd Inf Bde (41st Div) July 1917		
Miscellaneous	Cover for Documents Nature of Enclosures		
Miscellaneous	Headquarters, 41st Division. (2) A.	02/08/1917	02/08/1917
War Diary	La Roukloshille Area	01/07/1917	22/07/1917
War Diary	Westoutre	23/07/1917	31/07/1917
Miscellaneous	Verbal Messages Night Of 5/6 July		
Operation(al) Order(s)	122nd Infantry Brigade Order No. 127.	18/07/1917	18/07/1917
Miscellaneous	Administrative Arrangements For Forthcoming Operations Ref 122nd Infantry Brigade Order No 127	18/07/1917	18/07/1917
Miscellaneous	Appendix 'A'		
Miscellaneous	Appendix 'B'		
Miscellaneous	Appendix 'C'		
Miscellaneous	Brigade Instructions No. 4.	20/07/1917	20/07/1917
Miscellaneous	Brigade Instructions No. 5	20/07/1917	20/07/1917
Miscellaneous	Amendment To 122nd Infantry Brigade Instruction No. 4.	21/07/1917	21/07/1917
Miscellaneous	Addendum To 122nd Infantry Brigade Order No. 127	22/07/1917	22/07/1917
Miscellaneous	122nd Infantry Brigade Instructions. No. 1	22/07/1917	22/07/1917
Miscellaneous	Brigade Instructions No. 3.	22/07/1917	22/07/1917
Miscellaneous Diagram etc	Code Of Signals For Offensive Operations Only.		
Miscellaneous	Brigade Instructions No. 8.	22/07/1917	22/07/1917
Miscellaneous	Brigade Instructions No. 2.	24/07/1917	24/07/1917
Miscellaneous	Amendment To Brigade Instructions No. 2.	27/07/1917	27/07/1917
Miscellaneous	Brigade Instructions No. 7.	27/07/1917	27/07/1917
Miscellaneous	Table To Accompany Brigade Instructions No. 7.		
Miscellaneous	Brigade Instructions No. 9.	29/07/1917	29/07/1917
Miscellaneous	122nd Infantry Brigade Intelligence Summary	28/07/1917	28/07/1917

W095/2633/1

Vol. 8.

Headquarters
122nd Inf. Bde.
(41st Div.)
October 1917.

Army Form W.3091.

Cover for Documents.

Nature of Enclosures.

OPERATION ORDERS
****
45th Infantry Brigade

Notes, or Letters written.

CONFIDENTIAL.

Headquarters,
 41st Division.(A).

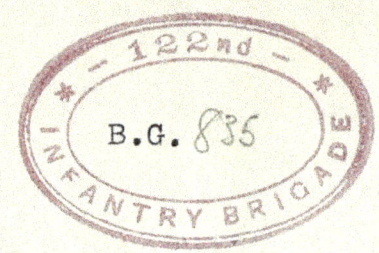

Herewith War Diaries of Headquarters and Units of the 122nd Infantry Brigade for month of OCTOBER 1917.

                                    Brigadier General.
                 Commanding 122nd Infantry Brigade.

7th November 1917.

Army Form C. 2118.

AO/122 Infy Bde

Vol /8

WAR DIARY
or
INTELLIGENCE SUMMARY.
(Erase heading not required.)

Instructions regarding War Diaries and Intelligence Summaries are contained in F. S. Regs., Part II. and the Staff Manual respectively. Title pages will be prepared in manuscript.

Place	Date October 1917.	Hour	Summary of Events and Information 122nd Infantry Brigade	Remarks and references to Appendices
LA PANNE.	1st		The Corps Commander, Lt.Gen. Sir J.P. DU CANE, K.C.B. Commanding XVth Corps rode round the back Area and watched Training.	
	2nd		The G.O.C. 41st Division addressed the Brigade and congratulated all ranks on their behaviour during recent operations.	
	3rd		Training according to Programme was carried out.	
	4th			
	4th		Brigade Warning Order for Move to Reserve Area issued.	App.1
	5th		Orders for move of the 122nd Infantry Brigade to the ST. IDESBALDE Area, being the Reserve Sector to the NIEUPORT BAINS SECTOR on the 7th October, issued.	App.2
	6th		Order referred to in App.2 is cancelled. Units of the Brigade being ordered to stand fast in their present Camps.	App.2a
	7th) 8th) 9th) 10th)		Training carried on.	
	11th		Orders received for Relief of Units of 124th Infantry Brigade by this Brigade on the COAST DEFENCE SECTOR.	
	12th		Brigade Order issued for move to COAST DEFENCE SECTOR.	App.3
	13th		Brigade Administrative Instructions for move to COAST DEFENCE SECTOR issued.	App.4
	14th 15th		122nd Infantry Brigade Headquarters close at LA PANNE and reopen at COXYDE BAINS. Relief was reported complete to Division at 4.55 p.m.	

J.Z.S

Army Form C. 2118.

WAR DIARY
or
INTELLIGENCE SUMMARY.
(Erase heading not required.)

Instructions regarding War Diaries and Intelligence Summaries are contained in F.S. Regs., Part II. and the Staff Manual respectively. Title pages will be prepared in manuscript.

Place	Date	Hour	Summary of Events and Information	Remarks and references to Appendices
	OCTOBER 1917.		122nd Infantry Brigade.	
COXYDE BAINS	16th) 17th) 18th)		Brigade established in the COAST DEFENCE SECTOR of which map is attached.	J.E.S
	19th		Captain I.E.SNELL, M.C. 1st Bn. BLACK WATCH assumes Brigade Majority vice Captain A.Y.GRAHAM THOMSON, M.C. Cameron Highlanders, to 15th Division to take up appointment of G.S.O.III.	
	22nd		G.O.C. and Staff Captain proceed to ENGLAND on leave. Lieut.-Colonel R.PENNELL, D.S.O. 18th Kings Royal Rifle Corps assumes Command of the Brigade during G.O.C's absence.	
	23rd		Copy of the Brigade COXYDE BAINS COAST DEFENCE SCHEME attached.	App.5
	24th) 25th)		No important events. Weather cold and stormy.	
	26th		Divisional Relief Order No.184 for the move of this Brigade to the NIEUPORT BAINS Sector of line.	
	27th		Divisional Relief Order No.184 cancelled. Divisional Warning Order for relief of 41st Division by 9th Division. received.	
	28th		122nd Infantry Brigade Warning Order for relief of this Brigade by the South African Infantry Brigade, 9th Division, in the COAST DEFENCE AREA on the 29th inst.	App.6
			41st Division Order No.185 for relief of 41st Division by 9th Division received. 122nd Infantry Brigade Order No.149 for relief of the Brigade by the South African Infantry Brigade, 9th Division, in COAST DEFENCE SECTOR, on 29th instant issued.	App.7
			All ranks recalled from leave, courses and employment outside the Division or Brigade.	
	29th		Dull day. 122nd Infantry Brigade was relieved by South African Infantry Brigade. Relief completed by 10 p.m. Brigade Headquarters opened in SYNTHE AREA G 12 B 1.6. at 4.30 p.m. Casualties Nil. Personnel of Brigade carried by bus.	J.E.S

Army Form C. 2118.

WAR DIARY
or
INTELLIGENCE SUMMARY.

(Erase heading not required.)

Instructions regarding War Diaries and Intelligence Summaries are contained in F. S. Regs., Part II. and the Staff Manual respectively. Title pages will be prepared in manuscript.

Place	Date	Hour	Summary of Events and Information	Remarks and references to Appendices
			122nd Infantry Brigade.	
SYNTHE AREA.	OCTOBER 1917. 30th		Day spent in refitting. Conference of Commanding Officers was held at Brigade Headquarters.	
	31st		G.O.C. returned from leave and reassumed Command of the Brigade. Units engaged in Route Marching. Conference at Divisional Headquarters at which G.O.C. Brigade attended.	

F. Worsley. Brigadier General.
Commanding 122nd Infantry Brigade.

6th November 1917.

SECRET. Copy No. 12

122nd INFANTRY BRIGADE WARNING ORDER No. 12.

1.- 41st Division (less Artillery) is relieving 42nd Division (less Artillery) in NIEUPORT BAINS SECTOR and COXYDE BAINS Coast Defence Sector.

2.- On the 6th and night of 6th/7th October the 123rd Infantry Brigade is relieving 127th Infantry Brigade in the line.

On 6th October 124th Infantry Brigade Group is relieving 125th Infantry Brigade Group in COXYDE BAINS Coast Defence Sector, relief to be completed by 12 noon.

3.- 122nd Infantry Brigade Group will march to ST. IDESBALD on 7th October and take over quarters of Brigade in Reserve.
Move will be completed by 11 a.m.
All personnel will move by beach and coast track between LA PANNE and ST. IDESBALD.

Headquarters 41st Division will close at LA PANNE and open at ST. IDESBALD at 10 a.m. October 7th.

4.- ACKNOWLEDGE.

Captain,
Brigade Major,
122nd Infantry Brigade.

4-10-17.

Issued to:-

Copy No.	
1	41st Division G.
2	12th East Surrey Regt.
3	15th Hampshire Regt.
4	11th Royal West Kent Regt.
5	18th Kings Royal Rifle Corps.
6	122nd Machine Gun Company.
7	122nd Trench Mortar Battery.
8	228th Field Company.
9	138th Field Ambulance.
10	No.2 Company Divsl. Train.

SECRET

S.C.G. 977

ADMINISTRATIVE INSTRUCTIONS
Reference 122nd Infantry Brigade Warning Order No.12.

1.- ACCOMMODATION.

On completion of relief the Division will be accommodated as shown in attached Schedule.

2.- S.A.A. - GRENADES.

Divisional Dump is at R 33 b 2.0.
Main Brigade Dump   M 14 c 2.2.
Additional Brigade Dump M 20 a 9.0.

3.- SUPPLIES.

Supply Railhead changes to ST. IDESBALDE (Light Railway) W 17 b 5.5. on 7th instant.

Supply Refilling Point and Fuel Dumps will be at W 17 b 5.5.

4.- WATER.

There is no difficulty regarding water in this area, numerous water points and horse troughs exist.

5.- ROADS and TRACKS.

The two roads OOST DUNKERQUE BAINS - NIEUPORT BAINS and OOST DUNKERQUE - M 20 d are both fit for wheeled traffic by day as far E. as OOST DUNKERQUE - OOST DUNKERQUE BAINS Road, and by night to near Battalion H.Q. at M 19 b 1.9. and M 20 b 8.4.
There are no tracks for transport.

6.- TRAMWAYS.

A map will be issued later showing light Railways and Tramways in the Divisional Area.
It is however more convenient under present circumstances to deliver both ammunition and rations by Horse Transport.

7.- MEDICAL.

A.D.S.   X 4 c 7.2.
            M 13 d 4.2.
Ambulance H.Q.   R 27 c 5.3.

8.- R.E. STORES.

Divisional Dump   X 8 d 3.8.
Advanced Dumps No.1 R 23 d 4.4.
                No.2 N 25 c 1.9.

9.- COOKING.

The Battalion in the line use Trench Cookhouses. No hot Food Containers yet available.

10.- ORDNANCE.

D.A.D.O.S. Store and Ordnance R.P. is at W 10 d 8.6.

11.- VETERINARY.

- 2 -

11.- VETERINARY.

No.52nd Mobile Veterinary Section will move to COXYDE BAINS in relief of No.19 Mobile Vet.Section 42nd Division on the 7th instant.

12.- SALVAGE.

Dumps are situated -

    Main Divisional Dump   - W 10 d 8.6.

    Brigade Dumps.   - X 1 a 2.9.
                                      R 27 c 5.5.

13.- BATHS.

Divisional Baths are at ST. IDESBALDE.
There are also some disused baths at OOST DUNKERQUE BAINS.

14.- ACKNOWLEDGE.

                                            Captain.
                                      Staff Captain.
                                  122nd Infantry Brigade.

5-10-17.

        Copy No. 1 Filed.
             No. 2 War Diary.
             No. 3 41st Division.
             No. 4 12th E.Surrey Regt.
             No. 5 15th Hants.Regt.
             No. 6 11th R.W.Kent Regt.
             No. 7 18th K.R.R.C.
             No. 8 122nd M.G.Company.
             No. 9 122nd T.M.Battery.
             No.10 138th Field Ambulance.
             No.11 No.2 Coy.Train.
             No.12 228th Field Coy.R.E.
             No.13 Brigade Major.
             No.14 Bde.Transport Officer.

SECRET

LOCATION OF UNITS 41st DIVISION.

UNIT.	Location.	Transport Lines.
Divisional H.Q.	ST. IDESBALDE.	With Unit.
C.R.E.	"	"
41st Signal Coy.	"	"
A.D.M.S.	"	"
D.A.D.V.S.	"	"
H.Q. Divisional Train.	"	"
D.A.D.O.S.	W 10 d 8.8.	
122nd Inf.Bde. H.Q.	W 10 d 7.3.	W 10 d 5.8.
1 Battalion.	W 10 d 3.7.	W 10 d 5.5.
1 Battalion.	W 11 c 3.6.	W 11 c 2.7.
1 Battalion.	W 5 c 1.1.	W 11 c 1.7.
1 Battalion.	W 10 b 4.7.	W 10 d 3.9.
122nd Machine Gun Coy.	W 6 a 6.4.	W 6 a 6.3.
122nd Trench Mortar Batty.	W 6 a 6.3.	
R.E.		
1 Field Company.	R 32 a 5.0.	R 31 d 6.5.
1 Field Company.	R 27 c 8.3.	R 27 c 8.3.
1 Field Company.	M 15 a 7.3.	R 27 c 6.2.
R.A.M.C.		
1 Field Ambulance.	X 25 b 7.8. (GROOTE KWINTE FARM)	With Unit.
1 Field Ambulance.	OOST DUNKERQUE BAINS.	
1 Field Ambulance.	ST. IDESBALDE.	
A.S.C.		
1 Company A.S.C.	W 18 c 5.9.	With Unit.
1 Company A.S.C.	W 18 a 2.5.	"
1 Company A.S.C.	W 18 a 2.5.	"
238th Div.Employment Coy.	ST. IDESBALDE.	
52nd Mobile Vet.Section.	COXYDE BAINS.	

....

6.- Billetting Parties for new area will meet Staff Captain at Area Commandant's Office, W 10 d 5.7., in ST. IDESBALD, at 3 p.m. on 6th October.

SECRET   Copy No. 2

122nd INFANTRY BRIGADE ORDER No.147.

Ref:- Sheet 11 S.E. (BELGIUM & FRANCE) 1/20,000.

1.- 122nd Infantry Brigade and No.2 Company 41st Divisional Train will March on the 7th October 1917 to the ST. IDESBALDE Area and become the Reserve Brigade to the NIEUPORT BAINS SECTOR.
Move to be complete by 11 a.m.

2.- Personnel will march in accordance with the attached March Table 'A' and the Transport in accordance with attached Table 'B'.

3.- Normal halts will be observed on the March and an interval of 200 yards will be maintained between Companies of Infantry, other Units, and Units' Transport.

4.- Baggage Wagons will report to Units on evening of 6th October.

5.- 6 Lorries for the Brigade have been applied for, and will be allotted as under:-
    Brigade Headquarters   1 lorry.
    Each Battalion   1   "
    Machine Gun Coy.   )
    Trench Mortar Battery.)   1   "
Lorries may be utilised for two trips.

7.- There will be no Refilling on Sunday.
Rations for consumption on Monday will be delivered on Sunday.
The 1 day's Reserve Rations now held by Units will then be dropped.
Refilling on Monday for consumption on Tuesday will be at 9 a.m. at No.2 Coy. 41st Div.Train's Camp at W 18 a 2.5.

8.- Brigade Headquarters will close at LA PANNE at 9 a.m. on 7th October, and re-open at W 10 d 7.3. at the same hour.

9.- ACKNOWLEDGE.

                                            Captain.
Issued at 7.30 p.m.   Brigade Major.
5th October 1917.   122nd Infantry Brigade.

Copy No.1 Filed.   No. 9 122nd T.M.Battery.
    No. 2 War Diary.   10 123rd Inf.Bde.
    No. 3 12th E.Surrey Regt.   11 124th Inf.Bde.
    No. 3 41st Division (G).   12 228th Field Coy.R.E.
    No. 5 15th Hants.Regt.   13 138th Field Amblce.
    No. 6 11th R.W.Kent Regt.   14 No.2 Coy.Div.Train.
    No. 7 18th K.R.R.Corps.   15 No.2 Sect. 41st Div.Sigs.
    No. 8 122nd M.G.Coy.   16 Transport Officer
              No.17 Staff Captain.

MARCH TABLE 'A'.

UNIT	FROM	TO	STARTING POINT	Time Head to pass S.T.	ROUTE.	REMARKS.
11th R.W.Kent Regt.	W 16 d	Camp W 11 c 3.1.	Head to leave Camp at 9 a.m.		By Coast Tracks	
8th E.Surrey Regt.	W 22 b	Camp W 10 b 4.7.	Head to leave Camp at 9.30 a.m.		-do-	
122nd T.M.Bty.(Personnel) LA PANNE		Camp W 6 a 6.5.	Street Junction W 14 b 4.2.	9.30 a.m.	By the Beach.	
122nd M.G.Coy.(Personnel) LA PANNE		Camp W 6 a 6.4.	-do-	9.35 a.m.	-do-	
122nd Bde.H.Q.(Personnel) LA PANNE)		W 10 d 7.3.	Bde.Signal Office	9.40 a.m.	-do-	
10th K.R.R.Corps.	BRAY DUNES.	Camp W 10 d 3.7.	Eastern end of BRAY DUNES Promenade V 27 c 3.0.	8.30 a.m.	-do-	
15th Hampshire Regt.	BRAY DUNES	Camp W 5 c 1.1.	-do-	9 a.m.	-do-	

TABLE 'B'

UNIT	FROM	TO	STARTING POINT	Time Head to pass S.T.	ROUTE.	REMARKS.
Transport of - 11th R.W.Kent Regt.	W 16 d	Camp W 11 c 3.1.	Cross Roads W 18 c 6.7.	9.30 a.m.	Via DE ZEEPANNE.	
12th E.Surrey Regt.	W 22 b	Camp W 10 b 4.7.	-do-	9.35 a.m.	-do-	
122nd M.G.Company.	LA PANNE	Camp W 6 a 6.4.	Cross Roads W 20 & 9.8.	8.45 a.m.	Via KERKEPANNE and DE ZEEPANNE.	
122nd Bde.H.Q.	LA PANNE	W 10 d 7.3.	-do-	9 a.m.	-do-	-so-
18th K.R.R.Corps.	BRAY DUNES.	Camp W 10 d 3.7.	Cross Roads D 9 a 7.6.	8 a.m.	Via WEST DAHHOEK - KERKEPANNE and DE ZEEPANNE.	
15th Hampshire Regt.	BRAY DUNES.	Camp W 5 c 1.1.	-do-	8.5 a.m.	-do-	-do-
No.2 Coy.Div.Train.	LA PANNE.	W 18 a 2.5.	Cross Roads W 20 & 9.8.	9.45 a.m.	Via KERKEPANNE.	

SECRET.   B.M.482.

War Diary

AMENDMENT TO 122nd. INFANTRY BRIGADE ORDER No. 147.

1.- Reference 122nd Infantry Brigade Order No. 147 dated 5.10.17., this move is now cancelled. All units of 122nd. Infantry Brigade will remain in their present Camps.

2.- Headquarters of 122nd. Inf. Bde. will remain at LA PANNE.

3.- ACKNOWLEDGE.

Issued at 6.30. p.m.
6th. October 1917.

A.T. Graham Thomson

Brigade Major,
122nd. Infantry Brigade.

Issued to all recipients of 122nd. Inf. Bde. Order No.147.

SECRET   Copy No. 4.

122nd INFANTRY BRIGADE WARNING ORDER No. 13.

1. 122nd Infantry Brigade will relieve the 124th Infantry Brigade in the COXYDE BAINS COAST DEFENCE SECTOR, on the 15th October 1917.
   Relief to be complete by 2 p.m.

2. Relief of Machine Gun Companies and Light Trench Mortar Batteries will take place on 14th and night 14th/15th October.

3. ACKNOWLEDGE.

                                        A. Y. Graham Thomson
                                                    Captain.
                                                 Brigade Major.
Issued at 7 p.m.   122nd Infantry Brigade.
11th October 1917.

                Copy No. 1 Filed.
                    No. 2 War Diary.
                    No. 3 41st Division.
                    No. 4 12th E.Surrey Regt.
                    No. 5 15th Hants.Regt.
                    No. 6 11th R.W.Kent Regt.
                    No. 7 18th K.R.R.C.
                    No. 8 122nd M.G.Coy.
                    No. 9 122nd T.M.Battery.
                    No.10 228th Field Coy.R.E.
                    No.11 138th Field Amblce.
                    No.12 No.2 Coy.41st Div.Train.
                    No.13 124th Inf.Bde.
                    No.14 No.2 Sect.41st Div.Signals.
                    No.15 Staff Captain.

War Diary

SECRET   Copy No. 2

122nd INFANTRY BRIGADE WARNING ORDER No.13.

1.- 122nd Infantry Brigade will relieve the 124th Infantry Brigade in the COXYDE BAINS COAST DEFENCE SECTOR, on the 15th October 1917.
   Relief to be complete by 2 p.m.

2.- Relief of Machine Gun Companies and Light Trench Mortar Batteries will take place on 14th and night 14th/15th October.

3.- ACKNOWLEDGE.

A. E. Graham Thomson
Captain.
Brigade Major.
122nd Infantry Brigade.

Issued at 7 p.m.
11th October 1917.

Copy No. 1 Filed.
No. 2 War Diary.
No. 3 41st Division.
No. 4 12th E.Surrey Regt.
No. 5 15th Hants.Regt.
No. 6 11th R.W.Kent Regt.
No. 7 18th K.R.R.C.
No. 8 122nd M.G.Coy.
No. 9 122nd T.M.Battery.
No.10 228th Field Coy.R.E.
No.11 138th Field Amblce.
No.12 No.2 Coy.41st Div.Train.
No.13 124th Inf.Bde.
No.14 No.2 Sect.41st Div.Signals.
No.15 Staff Captain.

SECRET   *War Diary* (3)   Copy No. 2

Ref. Sheet 11.S.E.   122nd INFANTRY BRIGADE ORDER No.148
1/20,000.
Sheet 19
1/40,000.

1.- 122nd Infantry Brigade will relieve the 124th Infantry Brigade in the HOXYDE BAINS Coast Defence Sector on the 14th and 15th October, in accordance with the attached Table of relief.
Relief to be complete by 4 p.m. 15th October.

2.- 124th Infantry Brigade is relieving 123rd Infantry Brigade in the line on 14th and 15th and night 15th/16th October.

3.- 122nd Machine Gun Company will, on 14th October, relieve 3 sections of 124th Machine Gun Company in the Coast Defence Area, and detach 1 Section to 124th Machine Gun Company, who will arrange for the section to take over from a section of 123rd Machine Gun Company in the line.

4.- The following representatives will be despatched to live with Units they are relieving 24 hours before relief:-

    122nd Inf.Bde.H.Q.　　　　Brigade Signalling Officer with a proportion of his personnel.

    From each Battalion -　　　1 Officer per Battalion, and 1 N.C.O. and 2 Runners per Company.

    122nd Machine Gun Company - 1 Officer from Company, 1 N.C.O. per Section, and 1 man per gun for 12 guns.
    (124th Inf.Bde. will send 1 N.C.O. and 4 men out of above up to the line with their representatives).

    122nd Trench Mortar Batty.- 1 Officer and 1 N.C.O.

5.- All details of relief will be arranged between Os.C. Units concerned.

6.- Units will take over Defence Schemes, Plans and Aeroplane Photographs, and Trench Stores, from the Units which they relieve. Copies of receipts for Trench Stores taken over will be sent to this office.

7.- Permanent Working Party of 400 men with 2nd Australian Tunnelling Company, on relief of a similar party from 123rd Infantry Brigade, will be found by Units on 15th October as under:-
    15th Hampshire Regt.　　　200.
    12th East Surrey Regt.　　100.
    11th Royal West Kent Regt. 100.
Details for this relief follow.
Present permanent Working Parties will be continued.

8.- Orders for Transport, and Administrative Instructions follow.

9.- Completion of relief will be notified to this office by code.

10.- Brigade Report Centre will close at LA PANNE at 2.30 p.m. 15th October, and re-open at COXYDE BAINS (W.6 b 6.5.) at the same hour.

11.- ACKNOWLEDGE.

Issued at 7 p.m.　　　　　　　　　　　　　　　　Captain.
12th October 1917.　　　　　　　　　　　　Brigade Major.
　　　　　　　　　　　　　　　　　　　122nd Infantry Brigade.

Copy No. 1 Filed.
No. 2 War Diary.
No. 3 41st Division.
No. 4 12th E.Surrey Regt.
No. 5 15th Hants.Regt.
No. 6 11th R.W.Kent Regt.
No. 7 18th K.R.R.C.
No. 8 122nd M.G.Coy.
No. 9 122nd T.M.Battery.
No.10 123rd Inf.Bde.
No.11 124th Inf.Bde.
No.12 228th Field Coy.R.E.
No.13 No.2 Coy.41st Div.Train.
No.14 140th Field Ambulance.
No.15 No.2 Sect.41st Div.Sign.
No.16 Bde.Transport Officer.
No.17 Staff Captain.

MARCH TABLE TO ACCOMPANY 122nd INFANTRY BRIGADE ORDER No.140.

UNIT.	Date of Relief.	In Relief of.	Situated in.	ROUTE	REMARKS.
122nd Machine Gun Coy.	14th October.	124th Machine Gun Company.	H.Q. WILTSHIRE CAMP X 1 b 5.8. 8 Guns on COAST DEFENCE. 4 Guns in WILTSHIRE Camp in Reserve.	Via COXYDE - COXYDE BAINS.	Head to arrive WILTSHIRE CAMP at 12 noon. Relief to be complete by 2 p.m.
122nd Trench Mortar Battery.	-do-	124th Trench Mortar Battery.	WILTSHIRE CAMP. X 1 b 5.8.	-do-	Head to arrive WILTSHIRE CAMP at 2.30 p.m. Relief to be complete by 3 p.m.
12th East Surrey Regt.	15th October.	10th R.W.Surrey Regiment.	Right Battn.Sector. BELGIAN ROAD R 24 c to R 31 central.	Via COXYDE - COXYDE BAINS - OOST-DUNKERKE BAINS.	Head to arrive Bn.H.Q. R 27 c 6.4. at 10.30 a.m. Relief to be complete by 1.30 p.m.
11th Royal West Kent Regiment.	-do-	26th Royal Fusiliers.	Centre Battn.Sector. R.31 central to about W 10 c.	Via ST.IDESBALDE- COXYDE BAINS Coast road.	Head to arrive Bn.H.Q. W 6 a 5.4. at 12.30 p.m. Relief to be complete by 2 p.m.
15th Hampshire Regt.	-do-	32nd Royal Fusiliers.	Battn. in Reserve. WILTSHIRE CAMP X 1 b 5.8.	Via DE LEUGENAAR Cross Roads W 27 b 8. - NIEUPANNE - COXYDE - COXYDE BAINS.	Head to arrive Bn.H.Q. WILTSHIRE CAMP at 3 p.m. Relief to be complete by 4 p.m.
18th Kings Royal Rifle Corps.	-do-	21st Kings Royal Rifle Corps.	Left Battn.Sector. W 10 c to FRANCO- BELGIAN Boundary V 23 b.		Head to arrive Bn.H.Q. LA PANNE W 14 b 9.5. at 9.30 a.m. Relief to be complete by 11 a.m.

An Interval of 200 yds will be maintained between Inf.Companies, other units, and Units' Transport.

SECRET   S.C.H. 193

12th East Surrey Regt.   228th Field Coy.R.E.
15th Hampshire Regt.   140th Field Ambulance.
11th Royal West Kent Regt.   No.2 Coy.41st Div.Sig.
18th Kings Royal Rifle Corps.   Bde.Transport Officer
122nd Machine Gun Company.   ~~Staff Captain.~~ Brigade Major
122nd Trench Mortar Battery.   No.2 Coy.Train.
123rd Infantry Brigade.   File.
124th Infantry Brigade.   War Diary.

----

(4)

Reference 122nd INFANTRY BRIGADE ORDER No.14 dated 12th October 1917.

Transport Lines of Units in COAST DEFENCE AREAS are near the Camps, and will be taken over with the Camps from Units of / 124th Infantry Brigade.

Transport will March with Units.

6 Lorries have been asked for, and will be allotted as follows:-

    Each Battalion   1 Lorry.

    Machine Gun Coy.)
    Trench Mortar Batty.)   1 lorry.

    Brigade Headquarters.   1 lorry.

Baggage Wagons will report to Units on the afternoon of 14th October.

Please ACKNOWLEDGE.

13-10-1917.
                              Captain.
                             Staff Captain.
                122nd Infantry Brigade.

S E C R E T

12th East Surrey Regt.
15th Hampshire Regt.
11th Royal West Kent Regt.
18th Kings Royal Rifle Corps.
122nd Machine Gun Company.
122nd Trench Mortar Battery.

122nd INFANTRY BRIGADE WARNING ORDER No.14.
@@

1.- 122nd Infantry Brigade will probably relieve the 124th Infantry Brigade in the NIEUPORT BAINS SECTOR on the 31st and night 31st October/1st November, being relieved by the 123rd Infantry Brigade in COAST DEFENCE SECTOR.

2.- Relief of Machine Gun Companies and Light Trench Mortar Batteries will take place 24 hours in advance of the remainder of the Brigade.

3.- On relief the 18th Bn. King's Royal Rifle Corps will hold the front line in the Left Sub-sector with the 15th Bn. Hampshire Regiment in Support.

The 11th Bn. Royal West Kent Regiment will hold the front line in the Right Sub-sector, with the 12th Bn. East Surrey Regiment in Support.

4.- Officers Commanding Units will make arrangements to send Officers to reconnoitre the positions which they are to take over, before the relief takes place. Not more than 4 should be sent at any one time.

Officers visiting front line positions will report at Headquarters 124th Infantry Brigade before going round the line.

5.- ACKNOWLEDGE.

6.- There will be a Conference of Commanding Officers at Brigade Headquarters at 2.15 p.m. to-morrow, 26th instant.

J.E. Snell
Captain.
Brigade Major.
122nd Infantry Brigade.

25th October 1917.

SECRET   *War Diary*   Copy No. 2.

122nd INFANTRY BRIGADE WARNING ORDER No. 15.

1.- The 9th Division will relieve the 41st Division in the NIEUPORT BAINS Sector on the nights of the 28th/29th and 29th/30th October.

2.- The South African Infantry Brigade will relieve the 122nd Infantry Brigade in COXYDE BAINS Coast Defence Sector on the 29th inst.

3.- 122nd Infantry Brigade will proceed to SYNTHE AREA on relief.

4.- Detailed orders, and lorry arrangements will be issued later.

5.- ACKNOWLEDGE.

J. E. Buell
Captain.
Brigade Major.
122nd Infantry Brigade.

Issued at 7 a.m.
28th October 1917.

```
Copy No. 1 Filed.
     No. 2 War Diary.
     No. 3 41st Division.
     No. 4 12th E.Surrey Regt.
     No. 5 15th Hants.Regt.
     No. 6 11th R.W.Kent Regt.
     No. 7 18th K.R.R.C.
     No. 8 122nd M.G.Company.
     No. 9 122nd T.M.Battery.
     No.10 123rd Inf.Bde.
     No.11 124th Inf.Bde.
     No.12 228th Field Coy.R.E.
     No.13 No.2 Coy.Div.Train.
     No.14 138th Field Ambulance.
     No.15 No.2 Sect.41st Div.Sigs.
     No.16 Bde.Transport Officer.
     No.17 Staff Captain.
```

SECRET   War Diary   Copy No. 2....

122nd INFANTRY BRIGADE ORDER NO. 149

Ref:- Map Sheet – A – 1/100,000 and
Sheets 11, 12, 19 & 20 – 1/40,000.

1.- The 122nd Infantry Brigade, 41st Division will be relieved in the COAST DEFENCE SECTOR by the South African Infantry Brigade, 9th Division, on October 29th 1917.

2.- The personnel of the South African Brigade Group will move by lorry to the COAST DEFENCE SECTOR, leaving SYNTHE AREA at about 9 a.m. On relief the 122nd Infantry Brigade Group Personnel will move by lorry to SYNTHE AREA to billets vacated by the South African Infantry Brigade.

3.- Billeting Parties from all Units will rendezvous at Cross Roads COXYDE BAINS (W 6 a 9.6.) at 8 a.m. under Captain G.P.G. REAH, Intelligence Officer 122nd Infantry Brigade. The Party from 18th King's Royal Rifle Corps will wait for Captain REAH at Cross Roads in LA PANNE (W 20 b 9.8.)

4.- 18th Bn. King's Royal Rifle Corps will em-bus independently in LA PANNE, on relief by a Battalion of the South African Infantry Brigade.

5.- Other Units will em-bus on the road COXYDE - COXYDE BAINS - ST. IDESBALDE, under the following arrangements:-

On Relief by Units of the South African Infantry Brigade, Units will proceed to COXYDE BAINS and report to Staff Officer, 41st Division at Cross Roads W 6 a 9.6. who will detail busses for them.
Busses will proceed to PETIT SYNTHE Cross Roads G 18 b 4.9., where guides will meet them.
Battalions will de-bus independently.

6.- Units will be billetted in the SYNTHE AREA as follows:-

122nd Infantry Brigade Headquarters	- G 12 b 1.6.
12th Bn. East Surrey Regiment.	- COUDEKERQUE BRANCHE.
15th Bn. Hampshire Regiment.	- ST. POL - SUR MER.
11th Bn. Royal West Kent Regt.	- PETIT SYNTHE.
18th Bn. King's Royal Rifle Corps.	- GRANDE SYNTHE.
122nd Machine Gun Company.	- ?
122nd Trench Mortar Battery.	- ?
228th Field Company R.E.)	
140th Field Ambulance.)	- FORT MARDICK.
No.2 Company 41st Div.Train.	- ?

7.- Extra Transport.- Lorries will be available for blankets and a very small proportion of the surplus kits.
These blankets and kits will be stacked by Units on the side of COXYDE BAINS - ST. IDESBALDE ROAD, near W 6 a 9.6. by 9 a.m., and a small loading party of not more than 5 men per Battalion left in charge.
Embussing Staff Officer will then allot lorries.

ø

8.- SUPPLIES. 122nd Infantry Brigade Group will draw from ST. IDESBALDE for last time on 29th instant, for consumption on 30th inst., and for first time on 30th instant at LEFFRINCKHOUCKE for consumption 31st inst. onwards.

The unexpended portion of the day's rations will be carried on the man.

ø In addition 11th R.W.Kent Regt. will detail 1 Off. to superintend dumping & loading of this kit.   9.- On arrival/-

- 2 -

9.- On arrival in billeting area Units will send Guides to Brigade Headquarters, for the purpose of guiding the Ration Limbers to their respective Units.

10.- Transport. No.2 Company 41st Divl.Train and 1st line Transport will proceed to PETIT SYNTHE AREA by road in accordance with the attached March Table.

11.- Command of the COAST DEFENCE SECTOR will pass from the G.O.C. 122nd Infantry Brigade to the G.O.C. South African Infantry Brigade on completion of the Infantry Relief.
Advanced Brigade Headquarters will open at G 12 b 1.6. at 4.30 p.m.

12.- Completion of Reliefs and arrivals at destination will be at once wired or communicated to Brigade Headquarters by the quickest means.

13.- ACKNOWLEDGE.

J. E. Snell.
Captain.
Brigade Major.
122nd Infantry Brigade.

Issued at 11 p.m.
28th October 1917.

```
Copy No. 1 Filed.
     No.  2 War Diary.
     No.  3 41st Division (G).
     No.  4 12th E.Surrey Regt.
     No.  5 15th Hants.Regt.
     No.  6 11th R.W.Kent Regt.
     No.  7 18th K.R.R.C.
     No.  8 122nd M.G.Coy.
     No.  9 122nd T.M.Battery.
     No. 10 140th Field Ambulance.
     No. 11 228th Field Company R.E.
     No. 12 No.2 Coy.41st Div.Train.
     No. 13 South African Inf.Bde.
     No. 14 123rd Inf.Bde.
     No. 15 124th Inf.Bde.
     No. 16 G.O.C. 122nd Inf.Bde.
     No. 17 Staff Captain.
     No. 18 Transport Officer.
     No. 19 No.2 Sect.41st Div.Sigs.
```

MARCH TABLE TO ACCOMPANY 122nd INFANTRY BRIGADE ORDER No.149.

UNIT.	STARTING POINT.	TIME OF PASSING S.P.	ROUTE.	REMARKS.
11th Royal West Kent Regt.	Cross Roads COXYDE BAINS W 6 a 9.6.	12 Noon.	COXYDE BAINS - COXYDE - KERKEPANNE - LA PANNE - ADINKERKE - DUNKERKE.	
15th Hampshire Regiment.	-do-	12. 7 p.m.		
122nd Inf.Bde.H.Q.	-do-	12.14 p.m.		
122nd Machine Gun Coy.	-do-	12.19 p.m.		
12th East Surrey Regt.	-do-	12.26 p.m.		

18th Bn. Kings Royal Rifle Corps and 140th Field Ambulance will march independently, starting from their respective Transport Lines by 12 noon.

228th Field Company R.E. will March independently, but must be clear of COXYDE CROSS ROADS by 12.30 p.m.

No. 2 Company 41st Divisional Train, will march independently but will be clear of W 18 c 4.7. by 12.30 p.m.

Halts of 10 minutes will be made at each clock hour.

The usual distance between Units will be kept.

Horses should be watered and fed before starting.

SECRET   *War Diary*   Copy No. 2

122nd INFANTRY BRIGADE
COAST DEFENCE SCHEME.
COXYDE BAINS SECTOR.

Map Reference - Sheet 11 S.E. 1/20,000.

1.- **FRONTAGE.**

   (a) The Brigade is responsible for the Defence of the Coast from the ROUTE EOLIENNE, R 23 B 95.30 (inclusive) to the FRANCO-BELGIAN FRONTIER at V 23 D 30.50.

   (b) The Sector is divided into three sections - boundaries as follows:-

      OOST DUNKERKE BAINS (RIGHT) SECTION - from ROUTE EOLIENNE to R 31 Central (excl).

      ST. IDESBALDE (CENTRE) SECTION - from R 31 Central to Infantry Trench at W 9 D 90.90 (inclusive).

      LA PANNE (LEFT) SECTION - from W 9 D 90.90 to FRANCO-BELGIAN FRONTIER.

2.- **COMMAND.**

   1. The General Officer Commanding the COXYDE BAINS SECTOR is responsible to the Commander of the LEFT BRITISH DIVISION in the Line.

   2. All FRENCH Troops in the Sector are under the command of G.O.C., COXYDE BAINS SECTOR.

3.- **DESCRIPTION OF THE DEFENCES.**

   The defences consist of:-

   'A'   A continuous belt of barbed wire along the whole fore shore.

   'B'   Infantry Trenches at irregular intervals.

   'C'   M.G. Emplacements.

   'D'   Anti-aircraft Emplacements.

   'E'   FRENCH NAVAL BATTERIES.

LORRAINE	2.	160 m.m.	guns.
MARSEILLAISE	2.	140 m.m.	"
ELIZABETH.	2.	100 m.m.	"
GIRARD.	2.	100 m.m.	"
ST. LOUIS.	2.	100 m.m.	"

   'F'   Four FRENCH and 2 BELGIAN SEARCHLIGHTS.

   'G'   Four FRENCH Naval LOOK-OUT POSTS.

   'H'   1. 47 m.m.) French Guns manned by British Troops
            12. 37 m.m.)

4.- POLICY OF DEFENCE/-

- 2 -

4.- POLICY OF DEFENCE.

The general policy of Defence is as follows:-

(a) To hold the sector with a front line of M.G. Posts which are to be permanently manned.

(b) To hold a proportion of the Infantry (not exceeding 25%) ready for the reinforcement of the front line this is to be done by Platoons in Support.

(c) To keep the remainder of the Infantry as a striking force.

(d) To counter-attack the enemy at once, and to drive him into the sea, should he effect a landing. The role of the striking force will therefore be for counter-attack rather than for reinforcing the front line of Defence.

5.- DISTRIBUTION OF TROOPS.

SECTOR H.Q., Infantry Brigade H.Q., COXYDE BAINS
W 6 b 8.5.
H.Q. FRENCH COMMANDANT, COXYDE BAINS, R 31 C 1.4.
(VILLA SANS-GENE).

'A' OOST DUNKERKE BAINS SECTION.

Headquarters R 27 D 05.50.
Held by 1 Battalion, 1 Section Machine Gun Company and 1 Section Trench Mortar Battery.
The section is divided into 2 Sub-sections each held by 1 Company.

RIGHT Sub-section.   )
 Coy.H.Q. R 23 c 5.0.   ) Finding 6 L.G., 1 47 m.m.
LEFT Sub-section.   ) and 11 37 m.m. gun Posts.
 Coy.H.Q. R 32 A 8.3.   )

2 Companies billeted at SURREY CAMP R 31 D.

'B' ST. IDESBALDE SECTION.

Headquarters W 6 A 5.4.
Held by 1 Battalion and ½ Section Machine Gun Coy.
The section is divided into 2 Sub-sections each held by 1 company.

RIGHT Sub-section.   )
 Coy.H.Q. W 6 B 20.65.   ) Finding 10 L.G. and
LEFT Sub-section   ) 2 37 m.m. gun Posts.
 Coy.H.Q. W 10 B 1.4.   )

2 Companies in Reserve in COXYDE BAINS.

'C' LA PANNE SECTION.

Headquarters LA PANNE BAINS, VILLA des ANCRES,
W 14 B 9.6.
Held by 1 Battalion and ½ section Machine Gun Coy.
The section is divided into 2 Sub-sections each held by 1 company.
RIGHT Sub-section   )
 Coy.H.Q. W 14 b 9.6.   ) Finding 9 Infantry
LEFT Sub-section   ) and L.G. Posts.
 Coy.H.Q. W 19 A 7.8.   )

2 Companies in LA PANNE BAINS.

'D' RESERVE/-

'D' RESERVE.

    1 Battalion in WILTSHIRE CAMP X 1 B Central.
    3 Sections Trench Mortar Battery X 1 B 5.8.
    2 Sections Machine Gun Company R 31 D 8.4.

6.- ACTION IN CASE OF ATTACK.

(a) The garrisons of the Posts will repel the enemy by rifle, Machine Gun and Lewis Gun fire.

(b) The Supporting Platoons of front line Companies not actually attacked, will take up positions of readiness along the Dunes.

(c) Companies in Reserve will proceed to previously selected positions of readiness, and be prepared to counter-attack immediately.

(d) RESERVE BATTALION, 3 Sections L.T.M.Battery and 2 Sections Machine Gun Company, will stand to in vicinity of their billets and await further orders from Brigade.

7.- LOOK-OUTS AND ALARM SIGNALS.

1. The French Naval Authorities and H.M.Ships which lie off LA PANNE at night - 2 Monitors and 1 Destroyer - are responsible for the look-out over the sea.

2. The British Sentries and Infantry O.P's, are responsible for the look-out on the beach.

The alarm for an impending hostile landing is given as follows:-

(a) By telephone.
(b) By the Naval look-out posts burning white and green flares.
(c) By ships at sea sending up green and white rockets or 3 green Very Lights in succession.

Reference (a) the Signaller at the Post giving the alarm signal will call up H.Q. COAST DEFENCES and BUZZ 'RAID NEAR......POST......SECTION'.

In the event of an alarm when there is a jamb on the line, the reports to Brigade will be sent in strict rotation.

(a) In OOST-DUNKERKE BAINS SECTION, POST 18 will be given priority over POST 17, and POST 17 will be given priority over POST 16, and so on.

(b) In ST. IDESBALDE SECTION, POST 1 will have priority over POST 2, and POST 2 priority over POST 3 etc.

(c) In LA PANNE SECTION, POST 9 will have priority over POST 8, and POST 8 priority over POST 7.

8.- ANTI-AIRCRAFT DEFENCES.

A.A. Lewis Guns and Vickers Guns are mounted so as to form a continuous belt of fire along the Coast from ROUTE EOLIENNE R 23 B 9.3. to FRANCO-BELGIAN FRONTIER at V 23 D 3.5.
In addition two posts are mounted at WILTSHIRE CAMP X 1 B central.

9.- COMMUNICATIONS/-

- 4 -

9.- COMMUNICATIONS.

    1. The G.O.C., COAST DEFENCES is in telephone communication with all 4 Battalions, and the FRENCH COMMAND.

    2. Front Line Battalions are in telephone communication with their Companies, and Companies with their Posts, as under:-

    (A) OOST DUNKERKE BAINS SECTION.

        Battalion H.Q. to RIGHT COY.H.Q. & POSTS 2, 5, 13 and 17., and Bn. O.P.
        Visual between RIGHT COY.- BATTALION H.Q., BATTALION H.Q. to BRIGADE H.Q.

    (B) ST. IDESBALDE SECTION.

        Battalion H.Q. to all Coy.H.Q. and POSTS 1, 2, 3, 6A and 7A.

    (C) LA PANNE SECTION.

                      (No. 2 Post.
                      (TERLINCK HOTEL O.P.
                      (No. 4 Post.
        BATTALION H.Q. to (No. 7 "
                      (No. 8 "
                      (No. 9 "

        There is also visual communication from No. 9 and No. 7 POSTS to TERLINCK O.P.

    3. There is a French Wireless Station between COXYDE BAINS and ST. IDESBALDE.

10.- APPENDICES.

    'A' STANDING ORDERS.)
) attached.
    'B' BEACH ORDERS.   )

11.- ACKNOWLEDGE.

                                            Captain.
                                       Brigade Major.
23-10-1917.   122nd Infantry Brigade.

        Copy No. 1 Filed.
             No. 2 War Diary.
             No. 3 41st Division.
             No. 4 12th E.Surrey Regt.
             No. 5 15th Hants.Regt.
             No. 6 11th R.W.Kent Regt.
             No. 7 18th L.R.R.Corps.
             No. 8 122nd M.G.Company.
             No. 9 122nd T.M.Battery.
             No.10 123rd Inf.Bde.
             No.11 124th Inf.Bde.
             No.12 42nd Division (G).
             No.13 French Commandant, COXYDE BAINS.
             No.14 G.O.C.
             No.15 Staff Captain.

SECRET

122nd INFANTRY BRIGADE COAST DEFENCE SCHEME.

COXYDE BAINS SECTOR.

APPENDIX 'A'.

STANDING ORDERS.

1.- SENTRIES

Will be posed as follows:-

Nature of Post.	By Day.	By Night.
Machine Guns.) 37 m.m. Guns.) 47 m.m. Guns.)	One per gun. (One per 2 guns if in same shelter).	2 per gun. One on the look-out, and one sitting down within kicking distance.
Anti-Aircraft L.G. or M.G.	2 per gun (one of which need not be on the look-out).	No firing allowed unless the identity of the aeroplane is unmistakably revealed to be hostile.
Infantry and L.G. Posts.	Where look-outs are found, 2 men, i.e. one in lookout and one sitting near at hand, ready to act as a Runner.	2 per Post, one on the look-out, and one sitting down within kicking distance.

2.- LOOK-OUT POSTS.

The number of Look-out Posts by day per Company will not exceed two; exclusive of any A.A.Sentries. But during misty weather sentries as for night will be posted.

3.- PREPAREDNESS TO MOVE.

Reserve Companies of front line battalions will be ready to move at 2 hours notice by day and 10 minutes notice by night. Reserve Companies may sleep without their boots.

4.- WORK.

Battalions are responsible for the upkeep of the Trenches and Posts in their Sections, for the repair of the belt of wire in front of their position, and for the provision of adequate shelter for their posts.

5.- AMMUNITION.

1.- S.A.A.

(a) 12 Boxes will be at the disposal of each Company in the line and will be divided amongst the Posts in the Company Sector as considered necessary by the Officers in Command of the Posts.

(b) 10 Boxes will be kept at each Battalion H.Q. in the Line.

(c) Lewis Guns will each have 24 drums.

(d) Machine Guns will each have 14 filled belt boxes at each gun position.

2.- HAND GRENADES.

10 Boxes at each Battalion H.Q. in the Line.

Contd/-

APPENDIX 'A' (Contd).

5:- AMMUNITION (Contd.)

    3.- RIFLE GRENADES.

        (a) 2 boxes at each Company Headquarters in the line.

        (b) 6 boxes at each Battalion H.Q. in the line.

    4:- 37 m.m. and 47 m.m. guns will each have 300 rounds per gun.

6:- GAPS IN WIRE.

All permanent gaps will be provided with wired knife rests which will be placed across the gaps half an hour after sunset, and removed at sunrise.

7:- SITUATION REPORTS.

    1. Situation reports - as in Trenches - will be rendered to Brigade Headquarters by 3.15 a.m. and 3.15 p.m. daily.

    2. ALL unusual occurrences and anything of interest noticed will invariably be reported AT ONCE to Brigade Headquarters.

....

S E C R E T

122nd INFANTRY BRIGADE COAST DEFENCE SCHEME.

COXYDE BAINS SECTOR.

APPENDIX 'B'.

B E A C H   O R D E R S.

1.- All Beach Regulations westward from point W 5 b 6.0. will be carried out by police under the A.P.M. during daylight. Regimental Posts and Sentries will, in the area stated above, and in the hours stated, cease to perform any police duties, and confine themselves to watching for hostile landings. They will assist the police if called upon to do so, but not otherwise.

2.- Eastwards of board at point W 5 b 6.0. the beach by day will be under military control, and all posts and sentries will stop anyone going on the beach anywhere, except:-

    (a) Our own airmen, if forced to land, when all possible assistance will be rendered by Coast Defence Troops.

    (b) Intelligence Officers carrying a green flag on the handlebars of bicycle.

    (c) Signal linesmen (by day or night) wearing two Red runner arm bands in addition to the blue and white signal arm bands.

    (d) General Officers on duty, and Officers accompanying them, and O's.C.Coast Defence Battalions in their own areas.

3.- Between board at point W 5 b 6.0. and board at point at W 5 c 9.6. Officers on duty are allowed to ride but must keep close to the wire.

4.- Between board at point W 5 c 9.6. and point where main ST. IDESBALDE Road reaches the Beach at W 10 b 3.7. Officers may ride and individuals may bathe.

5.- From board at W 10 b 3.7. westwards to FRANCO-BELGIAN Boundary at W 23 d, formed bodies of Troops, bathing parties and horse exercise parties are allowed. They must however proceed to the beach by the track running just West of VILLA TOBOGGAN at W 10 a 8.3. and NOT by the main ST. IDESBALDE Road.

6.- MUSKETRY and M.G. practice will only be carried out E. of point W 5 b 6.0. except that :-
    1. That portion of the coast between Track just West of TOBOGGAN POST at W 10 A and the 4° Bne. in W 9 D., will be reserved daily for Musketry between the hours of 2 p.m. and 3.30 p.m.

    2. That portion of the coast between 2 Bne. at W 13 D 25/20 and 1° Bne. at V 24 b 30/30 will also be reserved for Musketry daily between the hours of 2 p.m. and 3.30 p.m.

In both cases the Unit using the Beach is responsible for measures of safety.

                                                                 7.- Bathing/-

- 2 -

7.- BATHING.

No bathing is permitted in front of the residence of the King of the Belgians (W 14 c 5.9. - W 13 d 0.2.) or in front of HOPITAL de L'OCEAN.
All bathers must wear drawers when bathing in front of LA PANNE PLAGE and within 500 yards of each end of LA PANNE PLAGE.

8.- Coast between W 10 b 3.7. and TOBOGGAN POST about W 10 a 8.3. will be reserved for troops of RIGHT DIVISION, in the mornings. Troops of LEFT (COAST DEFENCE) DIVISION, will give way accordingly.

9.- CARE OF DEFENCES.

No troops are allowed to cross the wire entanglement at any point except where gaps are cut, or to walk over any of the Defences, except on duty.

10.- NIGHT ORDERS.

1. By night the beach everywhere will be under military control during the hours of darkness. During this time the whole of the coast lying between the wire entanglement and the sea will be treated as NO MAN'S LAND, and persons entering it will be liable to be fired on. The sole exception will be LA PANNE SECTION where every person will be challenged twice, and if possible apprehended. If such person endeavours to evade apprehension after being challenged, he will be fired on as in other sections.

2. There will be NO firing by night, except in case of a hostile landing, or under circumstances as indicated in para.1.

11.- All sentries will at all times use their discretion in opening fire, particular care will be taken not to fire on British or Allied Aeroplanes that have to make a forced landing.

122. Inf. B.H.Q.
September 1917.

On His Majesty's Service.

SECRET

O i/c AOC Section
3rd Echelon

D.D.O.S.
FIFTH ARMY.
No. 73/14
Date 27/10/17

CONFIDENTIAL.

Headquarters,

    41st Division.(A).

BG 654

       Herewith War Diaries of Headquarters and Units of the 122nd Infantry Brigade for month of SEPTEMBER 1917.

                                    Brigadier General
                     Commanding 122nd Infantry Brigade

7th October 1917.

Army Form C. 2118

WAR DIARY
or
INTELLIGENCE SUMMARY

(Erase heading not required.)

Instructions regarding War Diaries and Intelligence Summaries are contained in F.S. Regs., Part II. and the Staff Manual respectively. Title Pages will be prepared in manuscript.

Place	Date	Hour	Summary of Events and Information	Remarks and references to Appendices
	September		122nd Infantry Brigade.	
BOISDINGHAM	1st) 2nd) 3rd) 4th) 5th) 6th) 7th)		Training continued. Units practicing the attack over the Brigade Area.	App.1.
	8th		Orders for Practice Attack issued, to take place on 10th September.	
	10th		A Practice Attack was carried out to-day in accordance with App.1., which was watched by the Corps and Divisional Commanders.	
	11th		Training.	
	12th		A second Practice Attack over the same ground as the one which took place on the 10th inst., was carried out before the Divisional Commander.	
	13th		Orders for the Brigade to move from BOISDINGHEM to the WALLEN-CAPPEL billeting area issued. Billeting parties from Units of the Brigade leave Headquarters at 10 a.m.	
	14th		The Brigade left BOISDINGHEM via ST.OMER for the LE NIEPPE area. Brigade Headquarters closing at BOISDINGHEM at 9 a.m. and opening at the CHATEAU LE NIEPPE at the same hour.	
	15th		March was continued from NIEPPE to LE ROUKLOSHILLE to-day.	
	16th		Continuation of march from LA ROUKLOSHILLE to MURRUMBIDGEE Camp area. 12th East Surrey Regt. and 15th Hampshire Regt. to CHIPPEWA, with 122nd Machine Gun Coy and 122nd Trench Mortar Battery. 15th Hampshire Regt. and 18th K.R.R. Corps to RIDGE WOOD.	
	17th		Units of 122nd Infantry Brigade proceeded to the line in accordance with Brigade Order No.139. Battalion Fronts being taken over by 18th K.R.R.Corps on Right and 15th Hampshire Regt on Left. Each Battalion taking over its front with 2 companies. The 12th E.Surrey Regt. and 11th R.W. Kent Regt., march to RIDGE WOOD Area in accordance with same order.	

Army Form C. 2118

WAR DIARY
or
INTELLIGENCE SUMMARY
(Erase heading not required.)

Instructions regarding War Diaries and Intelligence Summaries are contained in F. S. Regs., Part II. and the Staff Manual respectively. Title Pages will be prepared in manuscript.

Place	Date	Hour	Summary of Events and Information	Remarks and references to Appendices
	SEPTEMBER 1917		122nd Inf. Brigade	
HEDGE ST TUNNELS.	17th		Brigade Report Centre closes at LA CLYTTE Camp and re-opens at HEDGE ST. TUNNELS at 6 p.m. Command of the line passes to G.O.C. 122nd Inf.Bde. on completion of relief.	
	18th		Our harrassing fire on the enemy's lines and back areas drew a considerable amount of retaliation, the ground rearwards from a line BODMIN COPSE - CLONMEL COPSE being swept with fire at intervals during the day. At 6 a.m. and 8.30 p.m. Practice Barrages were put down along the whole Army Front and reports testified to their extreme efficiency, no gaps being reported.	
	19th		At 3 a.m. a barrage was put down on the Corps Front, which was good except for a gap, which was reported at the junction of the 23rd Division (on our left) and our own division. This was however remedied in time. The 12th East Surrey Regt. and 15th Hampshire Regt. having moved from the RIDGE WOOD AREA to LANKHOF FARM - LARCH WOOD AREA, proceeded to the assembly area. Owing to the darkness of the night the 12th East Surrey Regiment failed to arrive at their forming up tape having gone too far left in error, but were rescued by the Brigade Major, who conducted the very intricate operations of the forming up. An account of the Attack Day and subsequent Days is attached in App. 122nd Infantry Brigade Warning Order is given under App.A. and the various instructions relative to it are shown under Apps. A1 to 8. The 'in' and 'Out' messages received during the battle are collected under headings In X and Out Y respectively. Administrative Instructions are grouped under headings - Administrative Instructions 2, 2a, 2b.	
	23rd		Orders for Relief of this Brigade by the 110th Infantry Brigade received. Relief was carried out by means of guides from each of our shell-hole positions being at a rendezvous (Bde.H.Q.) and conducting parties ointhe incoming units to their shell-hole positions, and to our forward lines, where they existed.	
	24th		Relief was completed with the exception of the 122nd Machine Gun Company by 1 a.m. and units proceeded to RIDGE WOOD remaining there till 4 p.m. when they marched to OUDERDOM SIDING en route for CAESTRE whither a train was to convey them.	

Army Form C. 2118

WAR DIARY
or
INTELLIGENCE SUMMARY
(Erase heading not required.)

Instructions regarding War Diaries and Intelligence Summaries are contained in F. S. Regs., Part II. and the Staff Manual respectively. Title Pages will be prepared in manuscript.

Place	Date	Hour	Summary of Events and Information	Remarks and references to Appendices
			122nd Infantry Brigade.	
	September 1917			
CAESTRE.	25th		Arrival in CAESTRE was effected about 11 p.m. 24th inst., Units not being settled in Camp before midnight.	
			In the morning G.O.C. addressed all Units separately, congratulating all ranks on their fine behaviour and gallantry during recent operations. Orders for move to the TETEGHEM AREA issued with Administrative Instructions.	
	26th		Brigade remained in CAESTRE. G.O.C. inspects the Draft of HAMPSHIRE CARABINIERS.	
	27th		Brigade moved by Bus from CAESTRE to the UXEM - LEFFRINCOUKE AREA.	
LA PANNE.	28th		Brigade moved by march route to LE PANNE. The 18th K.R.R.Corps and 15th Hampshire Regt. being billeted in BRAY DUNES, the 12th East Surrey Regt and 11th R.W.Kent Regt. with affiliated Units in LA PANNE.	
	29th 30th		Re-organisation and arrangements for training were taken in hand.	
			O C T O B E R.	
	1st 2nd 3rd 4th 5th		Training carried out by Units.	
			The Divisional Commander inspected the Brigade and expressed his thanks and satisfaction for the behaviour of all ranks during the recent Operations.	
			7th October 1917.	
			Brigadier General. Commanding 122nd Infantry Brigade.	

S E C R E T. OPERATION ORDERS NO. 85   Copy No......
                        by Lieut. Col. A. C. Corfe, D.S.O.,
                        Commanding 11th Bn. "THE QUEEN'S OWN"
Ref. Map 27 A. S.E.   Royal West Kent Regt. (Lewisham).

                                    3rd September, 1917.

INTENTION.   A practice attack will be carried out by the Battn.
                tomorrow, Sept. 4th, with the 16th K.R.R.C. on the
                right, and the 15th Hants on the left.
                OBJECTIVE. Line of shell-holes and trench behind,
                to be called RED LINE, at Q.33.b. This will be manned
                by a party of the 13th E. Surrey Regt., representing
                the enemy.

FORMATION.   The Battalion will attack on a two Company front,
                with each Company on a two platoon front, in two
                lines.

                    "B" Company will be on the Right.
                    "D"   "   " "   "   " Left.
                    "C"   "   " "   " In Support.
                    "A"   "   " "   " In Reserve.
                    Blank S.A.A. will be used.

                "B" and "D" Companies will take and consolidate
                the RED LINE, and make strong points, reinforced by
                "A" and "C" Companies as situation demands.

BARRAGE.   There will be a creeping barrage, represented by
                Signallers with flags.
                Rate of advance - Lifts of 100 yards every 6 minutes.
                Flag men will run 100 yards each lift as quickly as
                possible.
                A standing barrage will also come down and will be
                represented by explosives.

SMOKE.   Smoke candles and smoke rifle grenades will be issued
                to Companies to facilitate   the capture of
                Machine Gun Emplacements, or strong points.

MACHINE GUNS.   Hostile Machine Guns will be represented by tapes
                laid along the arc of fire.

REPORTS.   All reports will be sent to Battalion Headquarters,
                position of which will be notified on the ground.

ZERO HOUR.   Zero Hour will be notified later.

                    (sgd) A. J. JIMENEZ, Captain & Adjutant,
                11th Bn. "THE QUEEN'S OWN" Royal West Kent Regt.
                                    (Lewisham).

                Copy No. 1. C.O.
                         2. 2nd In Com.
                         3. Adjt.
                         4. Asst. Adjt.
                         5. War Diary.
                         6. Office Copy.
                         7. O.C. "A" Coy.
                         8. O.C. "B" "
                         9. O.C. "C" "
                        10. O.C. "D" "
                        11. I.O.
                        12. L.G.O.
                        13. B.B.O.
                        14. Sig. Sgt.
                        15. T.O.
                        16. Q.M.
                        17. M.O.
                        18. A/R.S.M.

SECRET.

Ref: Map 57 A.S.E. & Maps issued.

OPERATION ORDER No. 86, Copy No. 6
by Lieut.Col.A.C. Corfe, D.S.O.,
Commanding 11th Bn. "THE QUEEN'S OWN"
Royal West Kent Regt. (Lewisham).

9th September, 1917.

1. INTENTION.	An attack will be carried out on 10.9.17 by 41st Division on enemy line from Q.35.d.00.35 inclusive, to road at R.31.c.30.35 inclusive. Imaginary troops of other Divisions will attack on each flank.
2. INFORMATION.	The enemy's main line of defence is on the line MORINGHEM - ST. OMER. In front of this line he occupies an area about 1,500 yards deep with shell-hole posts, machine gun nests, and Strong Points and an organised line of defence about 600 yards from our front line.
3.	The enemy's main line will be captured and a line beyond consolidated.
4.	The attack will be carried out by the 124th Infantry Brigade on the Right, and the 12nd Infantry Brigade on the Left. The 123rd Infantry Brigade will be in reserve. (Not on the ground).
5. OBJECTIVE.	There will be three objectives, as shown on ~~attached plan.~~ maps issued.

First Objective...... RED LINE.
~~Second~~ Objective..... BLUE LINE.
Third Objective...... GREEN LINE.

The 122nd Infantry Brigade will attack that part of each objective lying within the Brigade boundaries. The attack on the RED and BLUE LINES will be carried out by the 18th KING'S ROYAL RIFLE CORPS on the Right, and the 15th Bn. HAMPSHIRE REGIMENT on the Left. The attack on the GREEN LINE will be carried out by the 12th BN. EAST SURREY REGIMENT on the Right, and the 11th BN. ROYAL WEST KENT REGIMENT on the Left. General true bearing of attack is 75 degrees. The dividing lines between Brigades and between Battalions are shown on ~~attached plan.~~ maps issued. The 21st BN. KING'S ROYAL RIFLE CORPS, and 26th BN. ROYAL FUSILIERS will be on the Left of the 124th Infantry Brigade in the attack on the first two objectives and the final objective respectively.

6. ATTACK.	The attack will be made in depth, the leap frog method being followed. The Battalion will advance in rear of the 15th Hampshire Regiment and will be formed up and cross "NO MAN'S LAND" immediately after them. After crossing "NO MAN'S LAND" the Battalion will drop back to such a distance as will ensure that it does not become involved in the attack. The Battalion will assemble behind the BLUE LINE after its capture, then close up behind the Creeping Barrage and advance under it to attack and consolidate GREEN LINE.
7. FORMATION.	*LEFT. RIGHT.* First Wave, "C" and "B" Companies. Second Wave, "A" and "D" Companies. Companies will assault in depth, the assaulting Waves consisting of two platoons, the remaining platoons following as support or Company reserve. Each assaulting Wave from the time it advances under the Barrage is responsible for its own mopping up, it will consolidate on the gained objective.

P.T.O.

2.

7. FORMATION. (Contd.).		Supporting and Reserve Platoons will consolidate in each case on a line in rear of the latter, thus giving depth to the defence.
8.		O.C. "D" Company will garrison after their capture by "B" Company Farm at W.6.a.50.95, TOWER HAMLETS Q.36.c.5.4. O.C. "A" Company will construct and garrison Strong Point at Q.36.a.00.70. Each of these garrisons will include one Lewis Gun.
9.		After capture of the Final Objective the new front line will be organised for defence as follows.- "C" and "B" Companies in front line N. of TOWER TRENCH including enemy Strong Point at Q.36.a.9.25. "A" and "D" Companies in support line about 100 yards S. of TOWER TRENCH with Strong Point at Q.36.a.00.70.
10.		Battalion will form up for attack on tapes immediately in rear of our front within the Brigade area by Zero minus ½ hour.
11.		Attack will be covered by artillery and machine gun barrage.
12. ZERO HOUR.		Zero hour 9.30 a.m. 10.9.17.
13. TIME TABLE.		Time Table of attack will be as under:-

Time	Zero	Description
9.30 a.m.	Zero hour.	Artillery Barrage comes down on line 150 yards in front of our front line. Assaulting lines move close up under it.
9.34 a.m.	Zero plus 4 mins.	Barrage will advance at rate of 100 yards in 6 minutes, closely followed by assaulting troops.
10.05 a.m.	Zero plus 35 "	Barrage lifts off RED LINE and latter is captured.
10.12 a.m.	Zero plus 42 "	Barrage halts 200 yards beyond RED LINE. Assaulting troops for BLUE LINE close up behind it.
10.28 a.m.	Zero plus 58 "	Barrage advances at rate of 100 yards in 8 minutes closely followed by assaulting troops for BLUE LINE
10.44 a.m.	Zero plus 1 hour 14 mins.	Barrage lifts off BLUE LINE and latter is captured.
11.00 a.m.	Zero plus 1 hour 30 mins.	Barrage halts 240 yards beyond BLUE LINE. Assaulting troops for GREEN LINE close up behind it.
11.15 a.m.	Zero plus 1 hour 45 mins.	Barrage advances at rate of 100 yards in 10 minutes closely followed by assaulting troops for GREEN LINE.
11.55 a.m.	Zero plus 2 hours 25 mins.	Barrage halts on GREEN LINE.
12.05 p.m.	Zero plus 2 hours 35 mins.	Barrage lifts from GREEN LINE. and latter is captured.
12.25 p.m.	Zero plus 2 hours 55 mins.	Barrage halts on final protective barrage 300 yards beyond GREEN LINE.

14. MACHINE GUN ETC.		The Battalion will be supported by one gun, Machine Gun Company, and one gun, 122nd Light Trench Mortar Battery, during the attack and consolidation.
15. CONTACT AEROPLANE.		Contact Aeroplane will fly over the area at the following times.-

    Zero plus 1 hour and 35 minutes.
    Zero plus 2 hours and 50 minutes.

Leading Infantry will light flares when called upon by the 'plane.

          Contd.

-3-

16.	COMMUNICATION.	The Brigade Signal Section will establish a forward station near each objective to be marked in each case by a blue and white flag. Units will open up communication with those stations.

        Battle Headquarters will be situated as under.-

        Divisional Headquarters. Road junction W.24.b.25.25.
        122nd Infantry Brigade) X.13.a.0.0.30
        Headquarters.)
        124th Infantry Brigade) .. ..
        Headquarters.)

17. DUMPS.   A Brigade Dump will be formed for S.A.A., Bombs, R.E. material and tools at W.12.b.7.2.

18. REGIMENTAL AID POSTS.   There will be Regimental Aid Posts at

        W.12.c.50.55.
        X.7.a.90.15.

19. SYNCHRONISING WATCHES.   Watches will be synchronised at 9 a.m. Sept.10th on the Assembly Area.

20. REPORTS.   O.C. Companies will render half hourly situation reports to Battalion Headquarters.

21.   O.C. "A" and "C" Companies will detail 1 Officer and 4 Other Ranks to keep touch with imaginary Battalions on Left.

        (sgd) A. J. JIMENEZ, Captain & Adjt.,
    11th-Bn. "THE QUEEN'S OWN" Royal West Kent Regt.
                              (Lewisham).

Copy No. 1. C.O.   11. L.G.C.
       2. 2nd in Comd 12. I.O.
       3. Adjt.   13. B.B.O.
       4. Asst.Adjt. 14. T.O.
       5. Office Copy. 15. M.O.
       6. War Diary. 16. Q.M.
       7. O.C. "A" Coy.17. A/R.S.M.
       8. O.C. "B" Coy.18. Sig.Sgt.
       9. O.C. "C" Coy.
     10. O.C. "D" Coy.

S E C R E T.

INSTRUCTIONS TO ACCOMPANY OPERATION ORDER No. 86 FOR PRACTICE ATTACK 10. 9. 17.

1. Kit will be carried as for operations on 7th June, 1917, except that Bombers and Lewis Gunners armed with rifles will carry 100 ~~yards~~ rounds S.A.A.

2. Consolidation will be carried out and trenches dug on the ground.

3. Special attention will be paid to reorganisation after the attack.

4. (a) Enemy dug-outs and Strong Points will be garrisoned by a skeleton enemy with blank ammunition. Sacks filled with straw will represent Germans and be treated accordingly.

   (b) Counter attacks may be expected.
   The enemy will be recognisable by reason of their wearing cloth caps reversed.

5. Battalions will arrange that 10% of their personnel, including Officers are made casualties.

   Casualties, except such as can be dealt with by Battalion Stretcher Bearers, will lie down for 30 minutes and then collect in rear at the Brigade Dump.
   An Officer will be specially detailed by the Brigade to collect such casualties.

6. The Creeping Barrage will be represented by men waving white flags.

7. Objectives, viz;, RED, GREEN, and BLUE Lines are marked by Flags of respective colours.

(sgd) A. J. JIMENEZ, Captain & Adjt.,
11th Bn. "THE QUEEN'S OWN" Royal West Kent Regt. (Lewisham).

SECRET.

Ref. Map ZILLEBEKE
6A. 1/10,000.

OPERATION ORDERS NO. 87,   Copy No. 4
by Lieut. Col. A.C. Corfe, D.S.O.,
Commanding 11th Bn. "THE QUEEN'S OWN"
Royal West Kent Regt. (Lewisham).

11th September, 1917.

1. **INTENTION.**

   (a). As part of a larger operation the 41st Division intends to attack, on a day to be notified later, from present British front line from J.25.b.2.1. to J.19.b.35.10 and capture enemy line from J.26.d.68.95 and J.21.c.92.75.

   (b). The 23rd Division and 39th Division are to attack on left and right of 41st Division, respectively.

   (c). The 122nd Infantry Brigade is to attack on left of Divisional front with the 124th Infantry Brigade on right and the 123rd Infantry Brigade in reserve.

2. **OBJECTIVES.**

   (a). There will be three objectives as shown on map.

       1st Objective........RED LINE.
       2nd Objective........BLUE LINE.
       3rd Objective........GREEN LINE.

   The 122nd Infantry Brigade is to attack that part of objective lying within Brigade boundaries.

   (b). The attack on RED and BLUE LINES will be carried out by the 18th King's Royal Rifle Corps on the right, and 15th Bn. Hampshire Regiment on left; that on GREEN LINE by 12th East Surrey Regiment on right, and 11th Bn. Royal West Kent Regiment on left.

   (c). General true bearing of attack 93 degrees.

   (d). The dividing lines between Brigades and Battalions is shown on map.

3. **FORMATION & METHOD OF ATTACK.**

   (a). The attack will be made in depth, the leap frog method being followed.

   (b). The Battalion will attack on a 2 Company Front, with 2 platoons of each Company in front line, the remaining platoons, or platoon per Company following behind as support or Company Reserve.
   The order of attack will be from right to left.-

       1st WAVE......... "B" Coy.   "C" Coy.
       2nd WAVE......... "D" Coy.   "A" Coy.

   (c). The Battalion will advance in this order behind 15th Bn. Hampshire Regiment at sufficient distance not to become involved in their attack, with the 12th East Surrey Regiment on the right.
   On capture of BLUE LINE they will assemble behind it, then close up under the barrage to attack the GREEN LINE which will be captured and consolidated by "B" and "C" Companies. "D" and "A" Companies will consolidate a line 200 to 300 yards in rear of GREEN LINE.
   The Supporting or Reserve Platoons of each Company will in all cases consolidate 150 yards in rear of their respective Companies giving depth to the defence.

   (d). Known enemy strong points for which special "mopping up" parties are necessary will be notified later. Apart from this each assaulting wave will be responsible for its own "mopping up."

P.T.O.

-2-

4.   C.C. "A" Company will detail one Officer and 10 other ranks for the special purpose of keeping in touch with troops of Brigade on left and their Battalion in touch with the situation.

5. BARRAGE. (a). The barrage will form at Zero on a line approximately 150 yards East of the present British Front Line. It will advance at Zero plus 4 minutes to a line 200 yards East of the RED LINE at a rate of 100 yards per 6 minutes. It will halt on this line for 30 minutes.

              (b). On resuming the advance, the barrage will move forward at 100 yards per 8 minutes to a line 200 yards East of and parallel to the BLUE LINE and will halt for 1 hour 30 minutes.

              (c). On resuming the advance, the barrage will move forward at a rate of 100 yards per 10 minutes to a line 200 yards East of and parallel to the GREEN LINE.

6. MACHINE GUNS. One section Machine Gun Company will support attack on and consolidation of GREEN LINE by this Battalion and the 12th East Surrey Regiment.

7. TRENCH MORTARS. One Stokes Gun under 2/Lieut. W.G.Leishman will be in support of and follow the Battalion.

8.   The following Light Signals will be used within the Brigade during the attack only:-

              (a) To be fired by an Officer only:-

                  Single White Very Light fired towards our original line to signify an Objective gained.

              (b). May be fired by any rank:-

                  Single Red Very Light fired in direction of suspected enemy Strong Point or Machine Gun holding up part of our line, for information of immediate supports.

9.   Assisted by 39th and 24th Divisions, the R.E. and Pioneers of the 41st Division are already at work preparing the Offensive Front.

10.   Further instructions will be issued on the following:-

              1. Artillery Instructions.
              2. R.E. and Pioneers.
              3. Signal Communications and instructions for contact aeroplanes.
              4. Machine Gun and Light Trench Mortar arrangements.
              5. Liaison.
              6. Administrative Instructions.
              7. Assembly.

              (sgd) R. KERR, Lieut. & A/Adjutant,
     11th Bn. "THE QUEEN'S OWN" Royal West Kent Regt. (Lewisham).

Copy No.			
1.C.O.	7.Off.Cy.		13.I.O.
2.2nd in Com.	8.O.C. "A"		14.B.B.O.
3.Adjt.	9.O.C. "B".		15.S.O.
4.A/Adjt.	10.O.C. "C".		16.T.O.
5.War Dy.	11.O.C. "D".		17.M.O.
6.R.S.M.	12.L.G.O.		18.Q.M.

War Diary

ADMINISTRATIVE ORDERS NO. I.
Reference O.C.87.

1. **S.A.A. & GRENADES.**
   - (a) Brigade Dump.   HEDGE ST.
   - (b) Battalion Dump.   J.19.c.4.2.
   - For all Battalions.   J.19.d.4.8.

2. **RATIONS.**
   - (a) Each man will start the attack with current days rations and the Iron Rations.
   - (b) No barrage rations will be dumped.

   Rations will be taken up daily as usual before the attack, except in the case of troops moving up on the night:- Attack Day minus 2/Attack Day minus 1, who will carry on the man rations for 2 days.

   To provide for the latter, the Supply Column will deliver 2 days rations on Attack Day minus 2, and NIL on Attack Day minus 1.

3. **R.E. STORES.**   Consolidation Stores.- J.19.&.2.5. (BODMIN COPSE).

4. **MEDICAL.**

   R.A.P.   J.19.c.4.3.
   (This will be shared by this Battalion and 15th Hampshire Regt.).

   ADVANCED COLLECTING POST.   HEDGE ST.

   COLLECTING POST.   LARCH WOOD.

   ADVANCED DRESSING STATIONS.   LOCK 8. VOORMEZEELE.

   MAIN DRESSING STATION. (Seriously Wounded).   CHIPPEWA, M.6.a.8.6.

   MAIN DRESSING STATION. (Lightly Wounded).   LA CLYTTE. N.7.c.4.5.

5. **WATER.**
   1. Forward Water Cart R.P. VOORMEZEELE.

      It is expected that 1,000 gallons per day will be available from bore holes at both :-
      - (a) MOUNT SORREL.
      - (b) HEDGE STREET.

   2. (i) 100 petrol tins for water will be issued to the Battalion to be dumped filled, in a place to be notified later.
      (122nd Trench Mortar Battery attached, may draw on these proportionately).

      (ii) 100 Petrol Tins will be on charge of Battalion Transport to enable fresh supplies to be brought up by pack.

   3. Divisional Water Dump is at LARCH WOOD.

(sgd) R. KERR, Lieut. and Adjutant,
11th Bn. "THE QUEEN'S OWN" Royal West Kent Regt.
(Lewisham).

S E C R E T.   MISCELLANEOUS INSTRUCTIONS
              Reference O.O. 67.

Ref: Map ZILLEBEKE
     6 A. 1/10,000.

1. **HEADQUARTERS.**   Headquarters at Zero Hour will be -

   (a) Battalion.   Dug-outs near J.19.c.50.15.
   (b) Brigade.   HEDGE ST. Tunnels.

2. **Ref. para.1.(b)**   The 68th Infantry Brigade will be on left of
   O.O.87.   122nd Infantry Brigade during the attack.

                         The 13th Durham Light Infantry will be on our
                         left for attack on GREEN LINE, with the 11th
                         Bn. Northumberland Fusiliers on the left of
                         15th Hampshire Regt.

3. **ARTILLERY.**   The attack will be preceded by a 7 days
                         Artillery preparation. During this period,
                         barrages in depth will be carried out to mislead
                         the enemy, cause him loss and destroy his shell
                         hole defences.

                         The infantry attack will be preceded by a barrage
                         of all natures of guns and howitzers, covering a
                         depth of about 1,000 yards. Known Strong Points
                         and ground from which the enemy could use Machine
                         Gun Fire with direct observation will be
                         specially dealt with, both by bombardment and
                         smoke screens.
                         Details of artillery barrage and times of lifts
                         will be issued later.

                         The attack of the Division will be covered by 5
                         Brigades R.F.A., organised in 3 groups.

4. **MACHINE GUN**   A Machine Gun barrage will be interposed in the
   BARRAGE.   Artillery barrage and certain batteries of Machine
                         Guns will be detailed to keep under fire localities
                         from which hostile machine guns may be expected
                         to hinder our advance.

                         Machine Gun barrage for 41st Division Front will
                         be provided as follows:-

                              238th Machine Gun Company.
                              2 Machine Gun Companies of 21st Division.

5. **Ref. para 3 (c)**   The ground captured by this Battalion will be
   O.O.87.   organised as under for defence :-

                         A front line about the GREEN LINE, with
                         Strong Points in rear of it. Position will
                         be chosen to gain observation down valley
                         W. of GHELUVELT.

                         Strong Points will be made by Battalion as under:-

                              Near J.21.c.5.6.
                         This will be constructed by "A" Company.

6. **ENEMY STRONG**   Enemy is known to have Strong Points in:-
   POINTS.(Ref.O.O.
   87,para.3 (d).   Ruin & Dug-out.   J.20.d.90.45.
                                                 ("B" Company front).

                         TOWER HAMLET CELLARS.   J.21.c.2.5.
                                                 ("B" & "C" Coys.front).

                         Dug-out.   J.21.c.75.30.("B" Coy
                                                              front).

                         Dug-out.   J.21.c.95.70.
                                                 ("C" Coy. front).

P.T.O

6. ENEMY STRONG POINTS.(Ref:O.O. 87. para. 3 (d). (Continues).	Special parties must be detailed to "mop up" as above.
7. Ref: para 4 O.O.87.	Party of 13th Durham Light Infantry will report to garrison of TOWER HAMLETS after capture, for liaison purposes.
8. ATTACK DAY.	The day on which Operations will be carried out will be designated the Attack Day. Zero Hour on Attack Day will be the exact hour at which the artillery barrage starts. After this hour references to times will be given in hours and minutes, a.m. or p.m., and not as heretofore.
9. PAPERS.	No papers dealing with this Operation will be taken forward of Brigade Headquarters when in the line.
10. DRESS.	Dress and equipment to be worn by all ranks will be as laid down in Section XXXI, S.S.135, paras. 1 and 2, with the following exceptions:-

    (a) Every 3rd man will carry an entrenching tool (1 pick to 3 shovels); men carrying these tools will not carry grubbers.

    (b) 150 rounds S.A.A. will be carried, except by Signallers, Scouts, Lewis Gunners, and carrying parties, who will only carry 50 rounds.

    (c) Bombers will carry 100 rounds S.A.A. and only 5 bombs.

    (d) Surplus kits to above will be left behind in packs which <u>must be clearly labelled with name and number of owner</u>.

(sgd) R. KERR, Lieut. & A/Adjutant,
11th Bn. "THE QUEEN'S OWN" Royal West Kent Regt. (Lewisham).

AMENDMENT TO OPERATION ORDER 87.

Delete para. 5 and substitute the following:-

(a) "At Zero hour the barrage will form about 150 yards in front of our front line where it will remain until Zero plus 3 minutes, while the Infantry form up close under it.
At Zero plus 3 minutes the barrage will move forward covering the first two hundred yards at a rate of 100 yards in 4 minutes and then proceeding at a rate of 100 yards in 6 minutes until it reaches a line 200 yards beyond the RED LINE. On this line the barrage halts for approximately 45 minutes.

(b). On moving forward the barrage will advance at a rate of 100 yards in 8 minutes until a line 200 yards beyond the BLUE LINE is reached. On this line barrage halts for approximately 2 hours.

(c) On resuming the advance, barrage will move forward at a rate of 100 yards in 8 minutes to a line 200 yards beyond the GREEN LINE, on which line the protective barrage forms. Infantry Posts will be pushed forward to a maximum distance of 100 yards in advance of the final line selected for consolidation.

(d) The portion of the creeping barrage nearest our own Infantry will be known as barrage "A", and this barrage will, on lifting off the RED, BLUE and GREEN LINES, contain a   proportion of Smoke Shell to indicate that the respective Objectives have been gained.

(e) Barrage "A" will pause 200 yards beyond the RED, BLUE and GREEN LINES, as shown in attached tracing to be superimposed on the ZILLEBEKE SHEET 1/10,000, edition 6A."

(sgd) R. KERR, Lieut. & A/Adjutant,
11th Bn. "THE QUEEN'S OWN" Royal West Kent Regt. (Lewisham).

Issued to all recipients of Operation Order No. 87.

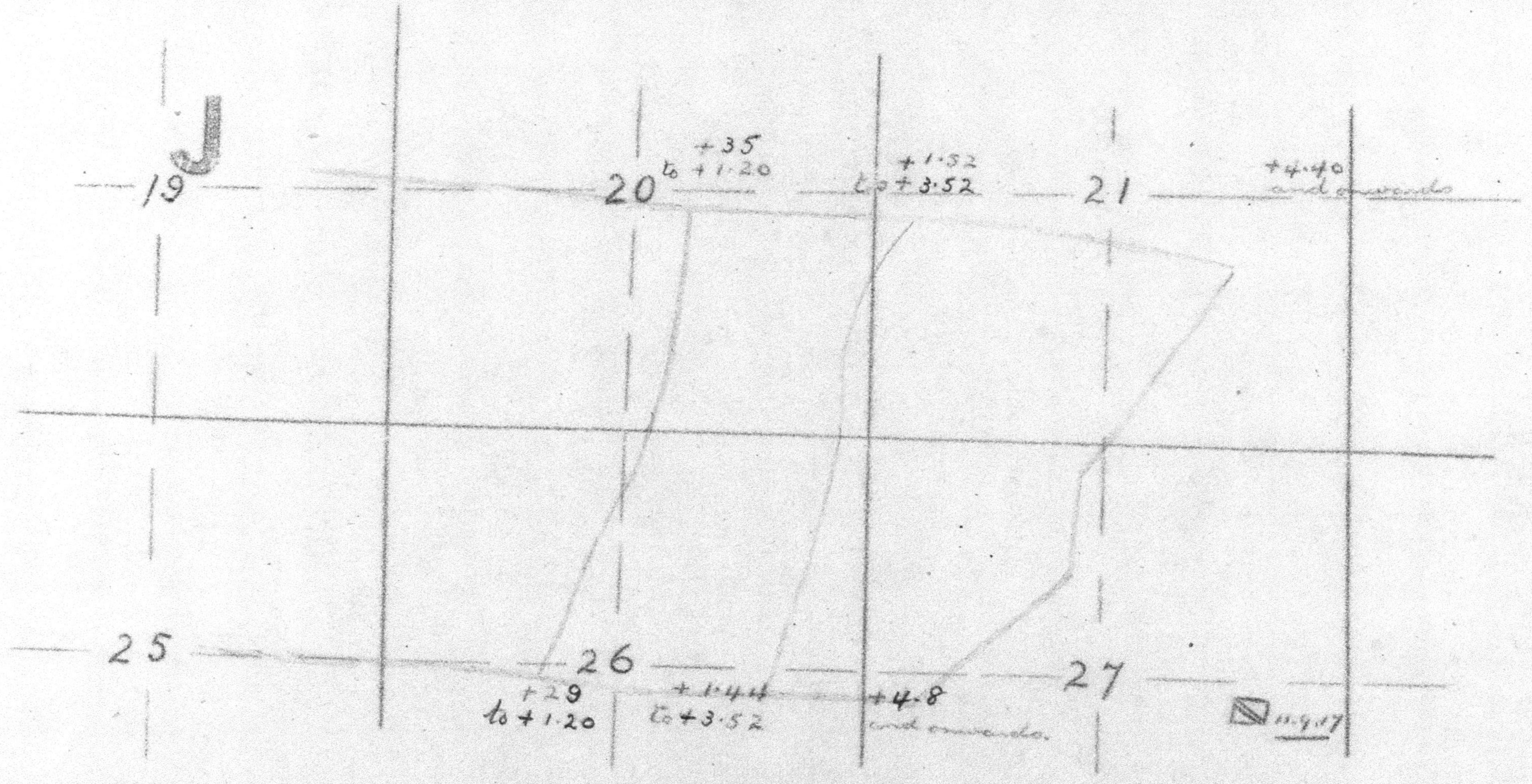
J
19
20
+35 to +1.20
+1.52 to +3.52
21
+4.40 and onwards
25
26
+29 to +1.20
+1.44 to +3.52
+4.8 and onwards
27
11.9.17

S E C R E T.

ADMINISTRATIVE ORDERS NO. 2.
Reference O.C. 87.

1. CLEARING THE BATTLE FIELD.
   (a). This will primarily be in charge of the Divisional Burial Officer, Lieut. E.S.L. GREAR, 23rd Middlesex Regiment.
   (b) O.C. Companies will render a return showing full particulars of all men buried by them, to Battalion Headquarters.

2. TRAFFIC.
   (a) The traffic circuits shown on map (which may be seen at Orderly Room) will be adhered to by all wheeled traffic in the forward area, subject to the following conditions:-

   (i) The Shrapnel Corner.- VERBRANDEN-ZILLEBEKE Road is not to be used by Transport on the day or night preceding, and the day or night of Attack Day.

   (ii) No transport except what is absolutely necessary is to move E. of the KRUISTRAAT HOEK - VIERSTRAAT Road on these two days and nights.

   (iii) Any Transport that has to proceed N. of the CANAL during the above period is to return by MIDDLESEX ROAD.

3. S.A.A., GRENADES, ETC.
   Particulars contained in Administrative Orders No.1. para. 1., are cancelled and the following substituted:-

   (a) Divisional Dump.   BARDENBRUG.
                              N.4.c.5.2.
   (b) Left Brigade Dump.   HEDGE STREET.
   (c) Battalion Dumps.   (J.19.c.4.2.
       (Left Brigade Sector). (J.25.a.5.9.
                              (J.19.d.4.6.

   A pack train will be organised by 122nd Infantry Brigade to be used for getting forward ammunition as soon as possible after ZERO.

   Each Battalion will supply 4 animals.

   This train will be commanded by an Officer of the 12th East Surrey Regiment and will be stationed near the BRICKSTACK I.33.a.2.1. ready to start after Zero hour.

   Of the 4 animals supplied by Battalions 3 will carry 2 boxes S.A.A. each, and one will carry 6 boxes Mills No.5 Grenades.
      This ammunition will be taken from Units Mobile Reserve.

4.
   S.A.A., Grenades, Sandbags, etc., will be issued to Companies as soon as drawn.

(sgd). R. KERR, Captain & A/Adjt.,
11th Bn. "THE QUEEN'S OWN" Royal West Kent Regt.
                                    (Lewisham).

Copy sent to all recipients
of Operation Orders No.87.

SECRET.

INSTRUCTIONS REFERENCE C.O.87 AND
MISCELLANEOUS INSTRUCTIONS TO C.O.87
DATED 11.9.17.

Some Map Reference.

1. **CONTACT AEROPLANE.** (1). A contact aeroplane will be maintained in the air from ZERO (if light enough) till ZERO plus 5 hours, 15 minutes.

    These aeroplanes will be distinguished by 3 broad white bands on the fuselage, and by the attachment of a black board to the left lower plane.

    They will be fitted with Wireless, but will only use it to report a counter-attack or transmit an Infantry message calling for a barrage.

    (2). Contact aeroplanes will call for flares by firing a white light and sounding a KLAXON HORN.

    Leading Infantry will light flares approximately at following times when called for by the aeroplane:-

    On RED LINE.   Zero plus 45 minutes.
    On BLUE LINE.   Zero plus 2 hours & 5 minutes.
    On GREEN LINE.   Zero plus 4 hours & 50 minutes.

    Any isolated parties on the flanks, out of touch, will also light flares when called on to do so.

    Colour of Flares........ RED.

    Lighting of flares should be supplemented by waving helmets, handkerchiefs, maps, etc., to attract attention from the 'plane.

    (3). A Wireless Aeroplane will be up throughout the day for the purpose of looking out for counter-attacks. In the event of a counter-attack developing this machine will call on the Artillery by Zone Call. The Zone Call will give the position and direction of the movement of the enemy's Infantry, and this information will be immediately communicated by the Artillery to the Infantry Brigades concerned. This machine will also transmit infantry messages calling for barrage.
    This machine will pay particular attention to the MENIN Road in the neighbourhood of GHELEVELT, and to the area immediately north and south of that place.

    (4). Brigade and Battalion Headquarters will have their ground signal sheets and call letters sewn on canvas. These will be kept rolled up and only exposed when the Contact aeroplane calls.

2. **SIGNAL COMMUNICATIONS.** (1). The 122nd Infantry Brigade will be in communication with Battalion Headquarters at J.25.a.3.9. and J.19.c.50.15 (BOW Headquarters) by buried cable.

    (2). The 122nd Infantry Brigade is establishing a Power Buzzer and Amplifier Station at I.30.b.5.7. and in present front line at J.19.d.4.5.

P.T.O.

2. SIGNAL COMMUNICATIONS. (Contd.).

(3). From before ZERO Hour the 15th Hampshire Regiment will lay and maintain 2 overground twin lines from cable head J.19.c.50.15 to J.19.d.4.5.

(4). A Divisional Visual Station (Call "H.S.") is being established at I.30.b.5.7. for receiving messages from Brigade Forward parties during the attack.

(5). The Brigade forward parties will be divided into 2 detachments, "A" and "B" under Lieut. D. WALKER, 12th East Surrey Regiment and 2/Lieut. S. LASENBY, 15th Hampshire Regiment.

(6). "B" detachment will assemble with the 12th East Surrey Regiment and this Battalion for attack on GREEN LINE.
They will go forward with them, moving along the ground cable laid by "A" detachment. At J.20.d.95.40 "B" detachment will join their cables to those of "A" detachment and will move forward with the third wave of the attack, dropping a Runner Relay Post at J.20.d.60.25, and establishing themselves finally at J.21.a.15.90. The aeroplane party and equipment of "A" Detachment will move forward with "B" Detachment on arrival of the latter.
"B" Detachment will endeavour to maintain the following communications from its final position.-

(i) By telephone.
(ii) By Power Buzzer to Amplifier at J.19.d.4.5.
(iii) By Visual to the Divnl. Station at I.30.b.5.7.
(iv) By pigeon.
(v) By Runner via Relay Posts at J.20.d.60.25, J.20.d.05.40, J.20.c.30.50, J.19.d.40.50.
(vi) By aeroplane communication.

(7). The new three letter code calls will not be used at present; the aeroplane calls will be used by all units.
The attached message code will be employed for visual, aeroplane, and power buzzer messages.

(8). S.O.S. Rockets are kept by the Brigade Forward parties, and Battalion Commanders may order the Brigade Forward parties to fire these, should the occasion arise.

(9). Instructions as to the number of pigeons available and where they will be drawn will be issued later.
Pigeons will be flown singly and not in pairs as heretofore.

(10). A Forward Dump of Signal Stores will be established in CANADA TUNNELS. Any Unit may draw stores from this dump after Zero Hour, on an Officers receipt.

(11). The responsibility for lateral communication is from Right to left.

Contd.

-4-

(6) (Contd.).

(i). An 18-pdr. barrage 300 yards beyond the GREEN LINE. This barrage will continue till Zero plus 6 hours 3 minutes, with a pause of 30 minutes from Zero plus 5 hours 18 minutes to Zero plus 5 hours 48 minutes, and a pause of 1¾ hours from Zero plus 6 hours 3 minutes to Zero plus 7 hours 48 minutes.

(ii). A Barrage in depth of all natures of Hows. up to 9.2" Hows. and 60-pdr. guns beyond the 18-pdr barrage. This barrage continues until Zero plus 6 hours 3 minutes, with a pause of 1 hour from Zero plus 5 hours 33 minutes, and a pause of 1 hour from Zero plus 7 hours 18 minutes to Zero plus 8 hours 18 minutes.

This barrage searches forward to a depth of 1,500 yards and at intervals by lifts of 100 yards.

(7). The "Starting Point" referred to in all preparatory Barrages is the following line:-

J.20.a.15.05 along line B B (Map Z) to J.19.d.98.38 - thence to J.26.a.03.60 to J.25.b.55.00.

4. MACHINE GUNS & TRENCH MORTARS.

(1). All orders relating to 122nd Machine Gun Coy. and Trench Mortar Battery are cancelled and the following substituted:-

(2). The attack will be supported by a Machine Gun Barrage under the Command of the Divisional Machine Gun Officer, 41st Division.
The Companies forming the barrage will be:-

238th
62nd
and 64th.

(3). One Section 122nd Machine Gun Company has been placed at disposal of Divisional Machine Gun Officer for purpose of work prior to Attack Day.

(4). Whole of 122nd Machine Gun Company will be at disposal of 122nd Infantry Brigade for the attack.
Support for capture and consolidation of GREEN LINE is as under:-

"One Section and One Sub-Section will follow rear Companies of Battalions assaulting the GREEN LINE and will come into action on capture of the BLUE LINE as under:-
One Sub-Section (2 guns) will follow rear Coys. of 12th East Surrey Regiment, and take up positions about J.20.d.65.15 firing North and South East to South. Two Sub-sections will follow 11th R.W.Kent Regiment,- Two guns will take up positions about J.20.d.90.50 firing N. N.E. (having all-round traverses).
Two guns will take up positions about J.21.c.3.4. firing N.E. (having all-round traverses).

(5). (a). 122nd Trench Mortar Battery will detail one gun to accompany each Battalion 122nd Infantry Brigade. He will arrange with O.C.Battalions for teams with guns to join Battalions prior to Assembly.
Forty rounds will be carried forward with each gun. Battalions concerned will supply necessary carrying parties.

3. ARTILLERY.   (1) Reference "Miscellaneous Instructions", para. 3.-

(a) Practice Artillery barrages accompanied by Machine Gun Fire will be carried out as under.-

Sept.15th. (41st and 39th Divisions Front.   8 a.m.
           (Xth Corps Front.   4 p.m.

Sept.16th. (Whole Army Front.   10 a.m.
           (41st & 39th Divisions Front.   6 p.m.

Sept.17th. (Xth Corps Front.   5.30 a.m.
           (41st & 23rd Divisions Front.   3 p.m.

Sept.18th. (Whole Army Front.   6 a.m.
           ("   "   "   8.30 p.m.

Sept.19th. (23rd Division Front.   11 a.m.
           (Xth Corps Front.   3 p.m.

(b) These barrages will normally consist of 4 barrages "A", "B", "D", "E" in that order, "A" being nearest our own Infantry.

"A" consists of 2/3rds available 18-pdrs.
"B"   "   "   1/3rd   "   and all 4.5" Hows.
"D"   "   "   6" Hows.
"E"   "   "   8" and 9.2" Hows.

(c) These barrages will all "creep". Rate of movement will be 100 yards every 3 minutes.

Necessary precautions for safety will be taken by Working Parties, Troops in the Line, and parties visiting the line.

(2). A Machine Gun Barrage will be interposed in these practice barrages under orders of the Divisional Machine Gun Officer.

(3). Harrassing fire will be carried out by the Field artillery and destructive fire by the Heavy Artillery, during the period of preliminary bombardment.
There will be gas bombardments, special day and night tasks, wire cutting, and "sprays" to keep the wire open.

(4). The Field Artillery will be organised in three groups, of which the Northern Group consisting of 6 18-pdr. batteries and one 4.5" How. Battery, under Lieut. Col. SUTTON, H.Q., LARCH WOOD, will cover 122nd Infantry Brigade. The Southern Group under Lt. Col. CARREN, will cover 124th Infantry Brigade.
SYMONDS Group under Lt.Col. SYMONDS H.Q. CANADA STREET, will be superimposed "Fleeting Opportunity" Group.

(5). The creeping barrage on Attack Day will be in depth as shown in para.1 (b) above.
Further details and pace of barrage will be as shown in "Amendment to O.O.87", already issued.

(6). (1). The final protective barrage on Attack Day will consist of:-

P.T.O.

4. MACHINE GUNS   (5). (b). The two guns with 12th East Surrey
      &   Regiment and 11th R.W. Kent Regiment
TRENCH MORTARS   will assist in capture of GREEN LINE and
(Contd.).   take up positions covering GREEN LINE after
                             its capture.

                          (sgd) R. KERR, Captain & A/AC.lt.,
                 11th Bn. "THE QUEEN'S OWN" Royal West Kent Regt.
                                  (Lewisham).

Copy issued to all recipients of O.O.87.

S E C R E T.   OPERATION ORDERS No. 86,   Copy No. 6
                by Lieut.Col.A.C. Corfe, D.S.O.,
Ref: Maps Sheet 27,   Commanding 11th Bn. "THE QUEEN'S OWN"
1/40,000, 27A S.E.   Royal West Kent Regt. (Lewisham).
1/20,000, Hazebrouck
5A 1/100,000.   13th September, 1917.

1. The 122nd Infantry Brigade Group will march to the WALLEN CAPPELL area tomorrow, and thence to ROUILOSHILLE area on September 15th.

2. Normal halts will be observed on the march. Tomorrow there will be a halt of 1 hour when head of column reaches level crossing at FORT ROUGE, 1½ miles E. of ARQUES.

3. On 14.9.17 (tomorrow) transport, less cookers, water carts & mess carts, will be brigaded under the Brigade Transport Officer. The Transport Officer will arrange for his transport to be at Cross Roads, LIHEUSE, en route for LE NIEPPE by 8.7 a.m. to take its place in the Brigade column.
On September 15th, Transport will accompany the Battalion.

4. Tomorrow 2 ambulances of 140th Field Ambulance will follow Infantry column.

5. The Battalion will parade on road outside "D" Coy. billet facing E. at 8.30 a.m. tomorrow.
Order of March - Band, "C" Coy., Headquarters, "A", "B", and "D" Companies.

6. DRESS.-
Fighting order, with waterproof sheets under flaps of haversacks. Only 100 rounds S.A.A. per man will be carried; the remainder will be handed to Quartermaster's Stores by 8 p.m. to-night.
Waterbottles must be filled.

7. One motor lorry will be provided to transport kits. This will be at Quartermaster's Stores by 8 a.m.

8. Packs, clearly labelled, will be stacked by Companies at Quartermaster's Stores, separately.
One man (preferably a man incapable of making a long march) per Company will report to the Quartermaster at 7.30 a.m. These men, under Sgt. T. Burnidge, will remain as a guard over the packs and act as loaders till the last load has been taken, when they will accompany the lorries on the last journey.

9. Officers kits will be stacked outside Quartermaster's Stores tomorrow by 7.30 a.m. to be packed.

10. One mess box per Company will be packed by 7.30 a.m.
Mess cart will call at each Company Mess about this time to collect them, and will be at Headquarters Mess by 7.45 a.m.

11. The Transport Officer will arrange with Lewis Gun Officer that Lewis Gun limbers are loaded to-night. The anti-aircraft Lewis Gun Guard will be dismounted at 6 a.m. in the morning and the gun packed.

12. Particular attention must be paid to march discipline.
Only the one man per Company, as in para.(8) will be allowed to ride by lorry.

13. Each cooker will immediately follow its Company; the mess cart and water carts will parade in rear of Battalion at 8.30 a.m.

14. M.O.'s cart and Orderly Room boxes will be packed and taken to Quartermaster's Stores by 6.45 a.m.

P.T.O.

15. The Battalion Guard will dismount at 6.a.m.

          (sgd) A. J. JIMENEZ, Captain & Adjutant,
11th Bn. "THE QUEEN'S OWN" Royal West Kent Regt. (Lewisham).

Copy No. 1. C.O.
       2. Sec. in Com.
       3. Adjt.
       4. Asst. Adjt.
       5. Off. Cpy.
       6. War Dy.
       7. O.C. "A"
       8. O.C. "B"
       9. O.C. "C"
     10. O.C. "D"
     11. L.G.O.
     12. I.O.
     13. S.O.
     14. B.B.C.
     15. T.O.
     16. M.O.
     17. Q.M.
     18. R.S.M.

CODE OF SIGNALS FOR OFFENSIVE OPERATIONS ONLY.

By Signal		Meaning
A	....	No signs of enemy ahead.
B	....	Enemy are retiring at..........
C	....	Held up by barrage at..........
D	....	Held up by Strong point at....
E	....	Enemy offering strong resistance at....
F	....	Further bombardment required.
G	....	Lengthen range....
H	....	Am in touch with Battalion on my right.
I	....	Raise Barrage.
J	....	Lower Barrage.
K	....	Have passed ....(Map Square).
L	....	Enemy apparently preparing to attack.
M	....	Short of Ammunition.
N	....	Barrage wanted at...............
O	....	Reinforcements wanted at........
P	....	Am in touch with Battalion on my Left.
Q	....	Am still advancing.
R	....	Artillery target at...............
S	....	Tank disabled at.................
T	....	Tanks have reached ....
U	....	Tanks required at ....
V	....	Short of water...................
W	....	Held up by Machine Gun fire....
X	....	Short of Grenades...
Y	....	Held up by wire at.............
Z		
O.K.	....	We are all right.

The Map location of the point of the line to which reference is made will be given, if necessary, by the clock code, the position of the sender being considered as the centre of the clock face and the hour 12 being always taken as pointing due North. The distance in yards from the point it is desired to describe will be given by a letter of the alphabet, A representing 50 yards; B 100 yards; C 200; D 300 and so on. The direction will be given by the hour on the imaginary clock face.

E.G. if it were necessary to ask for the the range to be lengthened at a point 400 yards North West of Battalion Hq. the message would be H H H E 10; H H H being acknowledged by T and the whole message by the code letters of the sender followed by R.D.

Distances of 150, 250 yards &c. will be given by a two letter signal, e.g. B A -150, C A - 250.

SECRET. OPERATION ORDERS No.88a. Copy No.....
by Lieut.Col.A.C.Corfe,D.S.O.,
Commanding 11th Bn."THE QUEEN'S OWN"
Royal West Kent Regt.(Lewisham).

15th September, 1917.

1. The Battalion will move to MURRUMBRIDGEE Area tomorrow, transport will accompany.

2. It will parade on rad outside Battalion Headquarters at 12.10 p.m. facing East in order - Headquarters, "D" Coy., Band, "C", "B", "A", Transport.

3. A distance of 50 yards between Companies will be observed.

4. Officers valises and men's packs will be stacked at Quartermaster's Stores by 10.30 a.m.
T.O. will arrange to collect Company mess boxes by 11.30 a.m. and Headquarters boxes by 11.45 a.m..

5. The usual party of 1 man per Company will accompany the boxes as loading party; the Divisional Commander's guard will also go in the lorries and get of at ZEVECOTEN.

6. The Billeting party of to-day will report to Lieut.R.O. RUSSELL at 8.30 a.m. with bicycles and 1 day's rations.

7. Billets will be left scrupulously clean and water bottles filled before moving off.

8. Parade States will be handed into Orderly Room by 10 a.m.

(sgd) R. KERR, Lieut. & A/Adjutant,
11th Bn."THE QUEEN'S OWN" Royal West Kent Regt.(Lewisham).

Copy No.1. C.O.   11. L.G.O.
        2. Sec.in Com.   12. I.O.
        3. Adjt.   13. S.O.
        4. Asst. Adjt.   14. B.B.O.
        5. War Dy.   15. T.O.
        6. Off.Cy.   16. M.O.
        7. O.C. "A".   17. Q.M.
        8. O.C. "B".   18. R.S.M.
        9. O.C. "C".
       10. O.C. "D".

S E C R E T. OPERATION ORDERS No. 89, Copy No. ....
                by Lieut.Col.A.C. Corfe, D.S.O.,
Ref: Map 28 S.W. N.W. Commanding 11th Bn. "THE QUEEN'S OWN"
& ZILLEBEKE.   Royal West Kent Regt. (Lewisham).

17th September, 1917.

1. Battalion, less Details, will march to RIDGE WOOD area this evening.

2. Parade on road outside CHIPPEWA CAMP at 6.40 p.m. Order – Headquarters, "A", "B", "C", and "D" Companies.

3. DRESS.– Fighting Order.

4. Platoons will march at 100 yards interval.

5. The Transport Officer will arrange for the following to call at the Camp:–
   (a) M.O.'s cart at   5.30 p.m.
   (b) Mess cart   "   5.30 p.m.
   (c) One Lewis Gun limber for Anti-aircraft gun at 6.15 p.m.
   (d) One limber for Officers trench bundles 6 p.m.
   (e) Horses for 2 cookers and 1 water cart. 6 p.m.

6. Remainder of Transport, viz. 2 Lewis Gun Limbers, bomb cart, S.A.A. carts, will be on OUDERDOM – MILLEKRUISSE Road about N.2.c.1½.1½. ready to join rear of the Battalion at 100 yards interval at 7.15 p.m.

7. Officers trench bundles must be stacked near Church Army Hut by 8 p.m.

8. All extra S.A.A., bombs, shovels, etc., will be issued at RIDGE WOOD tomorrow.

9. The Quartermaster will arrange with the Transport Officer for 100 petrol tins to be dumped at RIDGE WOOD.

10. All Officers valises, packs etc., of personnel proceeding to RIDGE WOOD must be stacked by Companies near Church Army Hut by 6 p.m.
    The R.S.M. will detail a guard from personnel left behind for above.
    The Quartermaster will arrange to collect above.

11. All Details left behind will parade at 7.15 p.m. and proceed to CARNARVON CAMP.

12. The Transport Officer will arrange for one cooker, one water-cart and one G.S. waggon to report here at 7 p.m. to proceed to CARNARVON CAMP.
    Valises of all officers left behind and Orderly Room boxes must be stacked by 7 p.m.

            (sgd) R. KERR, Captain & A/Adjutant,
    11th Bn. "THE QUEEN'S OWN" Royal West Kent Regt. (Lewisham).

        Copy No. 1. C.O.   11. L.G.O.
                 2. 2nd in Com.   12. I.O.
                 3. Adjt.   13. S.O.
                 4. Asst. Adjt.   14. B.B.O.
                 5. War Dy.   15. T.C.
                 6. Off. Cy.   16. M.O.
                 7. O.C. "A".   17. Q.M.
                 8. O.C. "B".   18. R.S.M.
                 9. O.C. "C".
                10. O.C. "D".

SECRET.   18th Bn. King's Royal Rifle Corps.   Copy No.

OPERATION ORDER No. 139.

Ref. Maps HAZEBROUCK 5A. and 27 S.E.

1. The 18th Bn. K.R.R.C. will move this afternoon, 16th September 1917, by route march to Camp at RIDGEWOOD.

2. The Battn. will be drawn up ready to march off, the head of the column on the road opposite the entrance to Battn. Hqrs., by 4.0 pm. Column will be formed in the following order:- "B", "C", "A", "D", Transport. Band between "C" and "A". "D" Coy. and the Transport will join the column when it is on the move.

3. Distance of 50 yds. between Coys. to be maintained, and normal halts observed.

4. Route will be via BERTHEN, WESTOUTRE, LA CLYTTE, and Overland Track. After passing BERTHEN the Battn. will come under the orders of the 124th Infantry Brigade for the march.

5. All officers' valises and mess stores will be collected from their Hqrs. They must be ready packed up at 2.15 pm.

6. The usual certificates will be obtained and forwarded to the Orderly Room.

7. Acknowledge.

                                    (Sd) H. W. Yoxall,
16.9.17.   Capt. a/Adjt.

Copy No. 1 Filed.
  "   2 War Diary.
  "   3   "
  "   4 O.C. "A" Coy.
  "   5 O.C. "B" "
  "   6 O.C. "C" "
  "   7 O.C. "D" "
  "   8 Transport Officer.
  "   9 Quartermaster.
  "   10 Signalling Officer.
  "   11 Medical Officer.

Secret   18th Bn KRRC.   Copy No.

Operation Order No 139.

1. The 18th Bn KRRC. will entrain at OUDERDOM station today 23-9-17.
2. Coys will parade in their own lines at 3-0 pm.
   Column of route will be formed in the following order - H.Qrs. A, B, C, D. Head of column will pass western edge of Cemetery at 3-20pm. Route via HALLEBAST.
3. Officers valises, mess stores - medical stores will be dumped by the cookers by 2-15pm.
4. Transport will proceed by road under special orders already issued.
5. O.C. Coys. will ensure that the camp is left in a clean & sanitary condition.
6. Acknowledge.

                 E.R.TAYLOR. Lieut
                 for Adjt. 18th KRRC

23-9-17.

Copy No. 1	Files	Copy No. 5	O.C. B. Coy
2	War Diary	6	" C "
3	" "	7	" D "
4	O.C. "A" Coy	8	T.O.
		9	M.O.

SECRET.   18th Bn. King's Royal Rifle Corps.   Copy No. 2

OPERATION ORDER No. 141.

Reference Map 27 S.E.

1. The 18th Bn. K.R.R.C., less Transport, will proceed by bus tomorrow, 27th September 1917, to UXEM, thence proceeding by route march to CONDEKERQUE.

2. All Officers' valises and mess stores must be ready stacked at the Q.M's. Store by 5.30 am.

3. The Q.M. will arrange for a guide to report to Brigade Headquarters at 7.0 am., 27th, to bring lorry to the Camp. Lorry must be returned to the S.M.T.O. from CONDEKERQUE in the evening of the 27th.

4. Rations for consumption on the 27th will be taken on the man. Men will carry their packs.

5. The Battn. will be drawn up in the following order, Hqrs. "A", "B", "C", "D", on the road leading from the Camp to the main CAESTRE - ST. SYLVESTRE CAPPEL road, with its head at Q.32 d.4.0.
   The Battn. will be divided into parties of 20 all ranks, with a distance of 8 yds. between parties. The Battn. will be in this formation ready to move off at 6.0 am.

6. Buses allotted to this Battn. are numbered 83 to 106. They will be numbered in chalk: numbers painted on them will be ignored.
   Bus No. 83 will be at Q.32 c.0.9, and head of the column will halt on the left-hand side of the road opposite this bus. Each party to the rear will halt in turn opposite its bus.

7. No one will embus until orders have been given by the Divisional Staff Officer directing embusment.

8. On arrival at UXEM no one will debus except under orders of the Divisional Staff Officer directing debusment.
   After the Battn. has debused it will form up at once, if possible clear of the road, and will not move until the buses are cleared.
   Guides will meet the Battn. at UXEM and lead it to CONDEKERQUE, a distance of 200 yds. will be maintained between Companies on the march.

9. Acknowledge.

                                           (Sd) H. W. Yoxall,
26.9.17.   Capt. a/Adjt.

Copy No. 1 Filed.
  "   2 War Diary.   Copy No. 8 Transport Officer.
  "   3   "   "   9 Quartermaster.
  "   4 O.C. "A" Coy.   "   10 Signalling Officer.
  "   5 O.C. "B" "   "   11 Medical Officer.
  "   6 O.C. "C" "
  "   7 O.C. "D" "

AQ 122 (Aerostic)
JB 16

August 1912

On His Majesty's Service.

CONFIDENTIAL.

GENERAL STAFF,
XVII CORPS.

CONFIDENTIAL.

B.G. 510.

Headquarters,

    41st Division.(A).

    Herewith War Diaries of Headquarters and Units of the 122nd Infantry Brigade for the month of AUGUST 1917.

[signature]
Capt

[signature] Brigadier General.
Commanding 122nd Infantry Brigade.

1-9-17.

PLEASE ACKNOWLEDGE

WAR DIARY
or
INTELLIGENCE SUMMARY

(Erase heading not required.)

Army Form C. 2118

Place	Date	Hour	Summary of Events and Information	Remarks and references to Appendices
SPOIL BANK	AUGUST 1st		122nd Infantry Brigade. The 'In' and 'Out' messages received during the Battle of the 31st July are included under Appendix 'A' for 'In' messages and "B" for "Out" messages. A Map marked "X Map" is given showing Barrage arrangements and Brigade Boundary and Objectives marked. A full report of the Battle is included under Appendix 'Z'. 18th K.R.R.Corps are relieved by 12th E.Surrey Regt. and brought back to Reserve Area.	A & B X.
	2nd		A considerable amount of shelling took place to-day. The SPOIL BANKS, WHITE CHATEAU WOODS, the CANAL BANKS and the RAVINE were all shelled at intervals.	
	3rd		The 15th Hampshire Regt. relieve the 11th R.W.Kent Regt. in the left Battalion sub-sector, the relief being completed in the early hours of the morning. The 18th K.R.R.C. are withdrawn to BOIS CONFLUENT and the 11th R.W.Kent Regt. take their place in the Sector Reserve area. A quieter day to-day. Shelling has been indiscriminate over the whole area.	
	4th		The quietest day we have had in the forward areas for some time, the left Battalion reporting that they had not been worried at all during the day. There was a certain amount of aerial activity on the part of the enemy.	
	5th		At 5.10 a.m. a message was received from our Right Battalion saying that the S.O.S. had been sent up, telephones had been cut, and they were in a dangerous position. The enemy counter-attacked our posts and was completely driven off. A report of this is included under appendix A report of the operations of the 31st July and subsequent days is attached under Appendix…. Later in the day the 15th Hampshire Regt. took over the Brigade front, and the 12th E.Surrey Regt. proceeded to BOIS CONFLUENT. At the same time a Composite Company was formed from the Brigade Details under Captain E.P.POWLES 18th K.R.R.C. This Company, 250 strong, was brought up into the Support area. The night was quiet till 9.30 p.m. when a message was received by our forward companies to say that the enemy was massing for an attack opposite HOLLEBEKE. A report of the operation is attached. Lt.Col. E.KNAPP, D.S.O. 12th East Surrey Regt. returns from leave.	2. 2.
	6th		A good deal of artillery activity on both sides to-day. The P & O Trench in BOIS CONFLUENT was shelled between 1 and 1.30 p.m. causing casualties to the 12th E.Surrey Regt. who were there. Otherwise the day was uneventful	3

Army Form C. 2118

WAR DIARY
or
INTELLIGENCE SUMMARY
(Erase heading not required.)

Instructions regarding War Diaries and Intelligence Summaries are contained in F. S. Regs., Part II. and the Staff Manual respectively. Title Pages will be prepared in manuscript.

Place	Date	Hour	Summary of Events and Information	Remarks and references to Appendices
			122nd INFANTRY BRIGADE	
SPOIL BANK	AUGUST 1917. 7th		A Shrapnel barrage was fired over FORRET FARM between 10 and 11 a.m. and our 5.9's were fired over the left of our from (N. of the CANAL). For the first time some Germans were seen, about P 7 & 8.8., they were fired on and apparently two of them were hit. Hostile fire seemed to be directed by a flag, which was raised from PUMP Fm (O 12 b). The STABLES of WHITE CHATEAU were shelled with 8", and SPOIL BANK was heavily shelled, both the entrances to this Brigade Headquarters being smashed in.	
	9th		At 8.20 p.m. a message was received from our Forward Battalion (15th Hampshire Regt.) to ask for S.O.S. over FORRET FARM. There was a heavy hostile barrage on FORRET FARM and OPTIC TRENCH. Our guns were fired at S.O.S. over FORRET FARM and a slow rate of fire was maintained over HOLLEBEKE. No infantry attack materialised and the fire dying down, everything was reported normal at 9.10 p.m.	@pp. 4
	10th		At 4.35 a.m. this morning under cover of a heavy mist barrage, we advanced our posts in front of HOLLEBEKE. A report of the operation is attached. Artillery activity was quieter except over SPOIL BANK which was as usual heavily shelled. One shell (though not actually penetrating) smashed in the roof of the Brigade Signal Office, it did not cause casualties however. The 15th Hampshire Regt. are relieved in the line by the 11th Royal West Kent Regt. and the 12th East Surrey Regt. The 11th R.W Kent Regt taking over the Left and centre posts,- the 12th E.Surrey Regt. the Right (FORRET FARM) post.	
	11th		The quietest day we have had in the forward area for some time. FORRET FARM and HOLLEBEKE were shelled at 3 p.m. And after 40 minutes, which it lasted, OPTIC TRENCH and OBLIQUE ROW were shelled with 4.2. Operations orders for relief of Brigade by 116th Infantry Brigade 39th Division on the 18/19th received. Brigade Relief Order re above issued.	5 6
	12th		Billetting order for the relief issued. Move order for the M.G.C. issued. Amendment to App.5 issued. Nothing of particular interest marked to-day.	7,7a. 8.
	13th 14th		The 122nd Infantry Brigade is relieved by units of the 116th Infantry Brigade 39th Division. The relief was not completed till the early hours of the morning when Command of the Sector passed to G.O.C. 116th Infantry Brigade.	

1875 Wt. W593/826 1,000,000 4/15 J.B.C. & A. A.D.S.S./Forms/C. 2118.

Army Form C. 2118

WAR DIARY
or
INTELLIGENCE SUMMARY
(Erase heading not required.)

Instructions regarding War Diaries and Intelligence Summaries are contained in F.S. Regs., Part II. and the Staff Manual respectively. Title Pages will be prepared in manuscript.

Place	Date 1917	Hour	122nd Infantry Brigade. Summary of Events and Information	Remarks and references to Appendices
ELZENWALLE	AUGUST 14th		On relief the Brigade moved back to the ELZENWALLE CAMP area preparatory to their move to training area. By 11.30 a.m. the entire Brigade was conveyed from HALLEBAST CORNER to the LA ROUKLOSHILLE training area in accordance with appendix 6.	
LA ROUKLO) SHILLE.	15th		Units bathed and began re-organisation.	
	16th		The G.O.C. Brigade inspected units and expressed his satisfaction with their behaviour during the recent operations. Orders for Army Commander's Inspection issued.	8.
	17th		The Corps Commander (Lieut.General Sir T.L.N.MORLAND, C.B.,C.M.G.,D.S.O.) and the Divisional Commander (Major General S.T.B. LAWFORD, C.B.) inspected the Brigade, drawn up for inspection in accordance with scheme.	9
	18th		Parade State for Army Commander's Inspection included in appendixes.	10
	19th		Orders for move of the Brigade to the NIEPPE-STAPLE Area issued. Billetting Parties left Brigade Headquarters at 3 p.m. to proceed to the new area.	10
NIEPPE.	20th		The 122nd Infantry Brigade arrived in the area referred to in App.11. Brigade Headquarters closing at LA ROUKLOSHILLE at 6 a.m. and opening at the CHATEAU NIEPPE at the same hour. Orders for move to the BOISDINGHAM AREA issued.	12
BOISDINGHAM	21st		The 122nd Infantry Brigade in accordance with Appendix 12 march to the BOISDINGHAM AREA, the Brigade Headquarters closing at Chateau NIEPPE at 10 a.m. and opening at BOISDINGHAM at the same hour.	
	24th		The Commander-in-Chief inspected the Division, orders for which are attached.	13
	25th) 26th)		Training is carried out by the Brigade units of Models being made of the new German shell hole Defence System for instructional purposes.	

27th/-

Army Form C. 2118

WAR DIARY
or
INTELLIGENCE SUMMARY
(Erase heading not required.)

Instructions regarding War Diaries and Intelligence Summaries are contained in F.S. Regs., Part II. and the Staff Manual respectively. Title Pages will be prepared in manuscript.

Place	Date	Hour	Summary of Events and Information	Remarks and references to Appendices
	AUGUST 1917.			
BOISDINGHAM	27th)			
	28th)			
	29th)		Training is carried out by units. Models being made of the new German Shell Hole Defence System, for instructional purposes.	
	30th)			
	31st)			
			Brigadier General.	
			Commanding 122nd Infantry Brigade.	
			1st September 1917.	

1875 Wt. W593/826 1,000,000 4/15 J.B.C. & A. A.D.S.S./Forms/C. 2118.

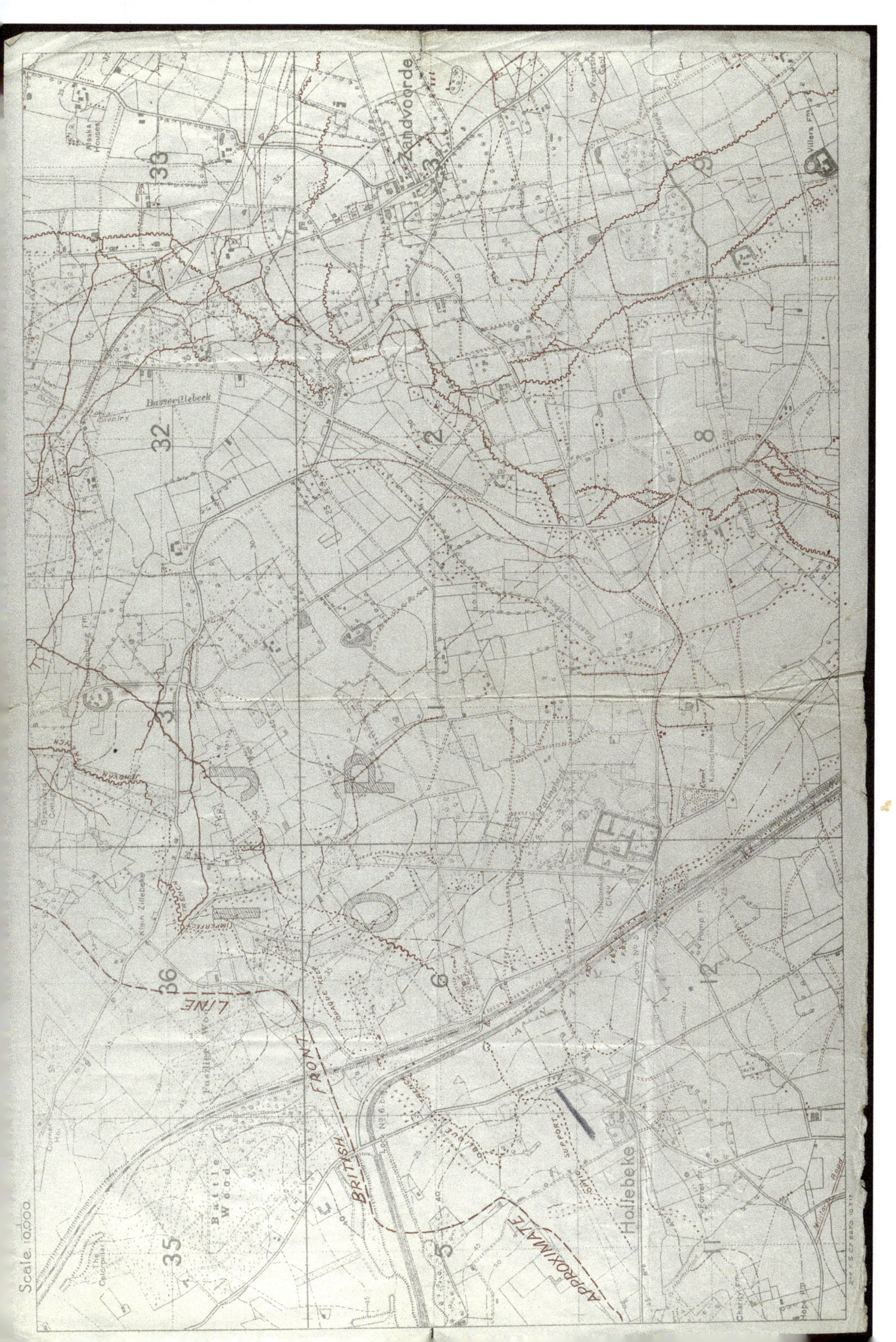

MESSAGE PAD.

41st Division.
Map reference or Mark on Map at back.

1. I am at .... and am consolidating,
   .... and have consolidated.
2. I am held up by M.G. at ....
3. I need :— Ammunition.   Water and rations.
            Bombs.   Very lights.
            Rifle Bombs.   Stokes shells.
4. Counter attack forming up at ....
5. I am in touch with Hants .... on Left at ....
6. I am not in touch on Right ....
7. Am being shelled from ....
8. Present strength. 1,070 .... rifles. Reinforcements required :—
   .... Platoons. .... Sections rifle bombers.
   .... Sections riflemen. .... Lewis gunners.
   .... ,,   bombers.
9. Hostile { Battery
            Machine Gun } active at Railway Embankment
           { Trench Mortar }

Time .... m.   Name. Dennell
Date 5-8-17   Platoon ....
                                        Company ....
                                        Battalion 12th ~~[illegible]~~ DAGGER

I.   Verbal Telephone Messages
          received on 5. VIII. 17.

5.15.   Verbal message from Hants to say
        that they had received verbal message
        from Surreys that the enemy had
        broken through — that Major Bennett
        and his Adjutant had gone forward to
        find out situation — Second in Command
        of Hants was also going forward.
        Thick mist — wires broken. except
        to Hants.

5.35.   Verbal message from M.G.C. reporting
        that runner had returned from Hollebeke
        and states that the enemy had crossed
        the Canal N.W of Hollebeke and had thus
        cut off the garrison.

5.40   Hants report message from man
        in E.5. Hollebeke surrounded.
        Runners by mounted up to OPAL
        RESERVE

5.55.   { M.G.C. report having received message
        { from   that Gunn shed two have
        { been captured.   ???

6.   Hants report that their front is
        apparently quiet — Message from
        Major Amery from old front line that
        situation O.K. these other patrols have
        gone forward to HOLLEBEKE

11

Last message repeated to Div" 6.3 a.m.

6.9. Div" forward report from 19th Div"
to the Effect that their left post had been
rushed — watch Right flank situation —

6.12 Rep⁴. to HAMLET. who
forward it to Major Aimey - who has
reported no M.G. fire in old front line

6.20. Communication with 87th Bde obtained —
Situation as far as known repeated to
them —
Reports situation on their left obscure
but all quiet elsewhere on their front

6.30 → Message from HAMLET rec'd from Hollebeke,
Two posts in Hollebeke lost —
Left still held — Situation still
obscure.
Rep⁴. Div" by wire.

6.45. Message from Dagger reporting that
situation was quite quiet, that apparently
operation was only a raid, & that our
line in HOLLEBEKE was secure.

6.50. 124 report small raid on their left
battalion of KLEINE ZILLEBEKE road.

6.50. Bow & Hammer "stand down".
Situation reported to 87 Bde. They report

111

this message from their left battalion stating that 100 Sturmtruppen had tried to shell their left post & had been driven out.

7.15. Message from M.G.C. stating that prisoner had been taken in or near HOLLEBEKE who states that a sturmtruppe 200 strong had been ordered to attack HOLLEBEKE and stay there (?). Was this sent to 57th Bde Hqrs. 209 on shoulder strap.

K. M.G.C. lost 2 guns in Village and 19th Divl. Coy. 1 gun.

7.25. Jagger reports capture of prisoner. 209 on shoulders with white edges to shoulder strap.

Unconfirmed report both Germans and British in HOLLEBEKE.

Repd. Divn.

7.40. Call from JAGGER. Message received from Major Pennell from ——— position W of HOLLEBEKE where he had 100 men, asking for reinforcements, amm. and bombs.

... OPAL RESERVE
B o o's
C new tablets
D OBLIQUE
ROW

Chemistry 1/day

from
To

inish
12 E.S.
15 Knife
16 Awl
18 Knife
122 M C's
122 TM B

7.45.	HAMLET told to send two platoons towards HOLLEBEKE with bombs to join Major Pennell
8.0	2 prisoners arrive. 209 + 213
8.5.	FORRET FM reported recaptured with 40-50 prisoners by enemy. Shooting coming from direction of Hollebeke.
8.10.	Sy Bdr asked to send two platoons to link up with our right and assist in any attack on HOLLEBEKE with flanking covering fire.
8.20.	Hants report Capt Fowler & part of his Coy still holding out on left HOLLEBEKE. Col C Barnard has seen Major Pennell & Hants Corps collected near Optic Support — One Coy has been sent to assist Major Pennell.
	Hants report FORRET FM in Enemy's hands, but apparently not in HOLLEBEKE.
	Surreys to attempt to clear up Village under cover of the mist.
9.35	Message from HAMLET. Artillery to lengthen 100. Getting in touch with DAGGER. Enemy reported retiring left front of HOLLEBEKE. Situation clearing. Col C Barnard has seen Major Pennell who was all right.
9.50.	Col Cary Barnard reports HOLLEBEKE now in our possession, also FORRET FARM —

Sunken Road — 1-50

Oak [?]

(12)

Kents ok.   Right
Surreys to Left Bn front.   left
Hants Support   2 Coys in OPAL Reserve
                                              & OBLIQUE ROW
                                                  & TRENCH
KRRC in Reserve   Behind DAMMSTRASSE

enemy massing in P.1.d.

9.55. 41 DA report enemy massing in O.12.a.

10.5a.
10.10 am. MGC report situation at 9.25 AM.
4 guns at O.4.a 95.45.
3 guns in OPAL RESERVE.
2 guns in line of O.5.c 90.70.

10.12.AM DMSO asked to put bursts of fire in O.12.a.

10.30 11a.11d.92.c Col. C.B. reports enemy forming in O.11.d.9.2.

10.40. Col. C.B. reports that he has one Coy at FERRET FM, and the remainder beyond HOLLEBEKE.

10.50. LOYALTY reported shelling from ZANDVOORDE Group. Counter battery informed.

11.30. Major Pennell reports having returned from HOLLEBEKE. Our troops now right in front of the village. Stretcher bearers required. 13 more prisoners reported. Heavy enemy casualties. Much sniping.

12.5 p. Col. C.B. is sending report from Capt Fowler. Hants consolidating in front of HOLLEBEKE. He wants details from Bas Confluent. Has moved back to original Headquarters.

SECRET War Diary   Copy No. 2

122nd INFANTRY BRIGADE ORDER No. 130

1. 15th Hampshire Regiment will take over the Brigade Front to-night August 5th/6th and establish their Headquarters at O 5 c 5.9.

2. 12th East Surrey Regiment as soon as 15th Hampshire Regiment have taken over, will assemble in BOIS CONFLUENT. Headquarters BOIS CONFLUENT.

3. Details as to relief and time to be arranged between Officers Commanding Units concerned.

4. 18th Kings Royal Rifle Corps will occupy area between OAK ROW and OLD GERMAN Front Line inclusive, less accommodation for 1 Platoon in OAK ROW.
Headquarters at LOCK HOUSE BANK TUNNELS.
(Accommodation for Company in LOCK HOUSE BANK TUNNELS not now available, but space for 30 men in NORFOLK ROAD TUNNEL.

5. A Composite Company under Captain E.P. POWLES 18th King's Royal Rifle Corps will arrive at SHELLEY DUMP by bus about 8 p.m. O.C.15th Hampshire Regt. will detail 4 Guides to be at SHELLEY DUMP at 7.30 p.m. and will arrange that the Company is accommodated as under -

   Company Headquarters.   BROKEN BRIDGE DUGOUTS   O 4 b 2.4.
   3 Platoons   OBLIQUE ROW and OPTIC TRENCH.
   1 Platoon   OAK ROW and WHITE CHATEAU.

6. 11th Royal West Kent Regt. will be withdrawn to WOOD CAMP. They will be conveyed by busses from SHELLEY DUMP at about 8 p.m.

7. Completion of moves and taking over of the line will be reported to this office.

8. ACKNOWLEDGE.

                                                Captain.
                                           Brigade Major.
Issued at 6.15 p.m.   122nd Infantry Brigade.
5-8-17.

              Copy No. 1 File
                   No. 2 War Diary.
                   No. 3 41st Div.(G)
                   No. 4 12th E.Surrey Regt.
                   No. 5 15th Hants.Regt.
                   No. 6 11th R.W.Kent Regt.
                   No. 7 18th K.R.R.C.
                   No. 8 122nd M.G.Company.
                   No. 9 124th Inf.Bde.
                   No.10 57th Inf.Bde.
                   No.11 228th Field Coy.
                   No.12 Capt. E.P. Powles.
                   No.13 Staff Captn.
                   No.14 Bde. Maj.
                   No.15 2 Sec. Div. Sigs.
                   No.16 T.M.Bty.

CONFIDENTIAL B.G.359

Headquarters,

   41st Division. (G).

122nd INFANTRY BRIGADE INTELLIGENCE SUMMARY
6 p.m. 5-8-17 to 6 a.m. 6-8-17.

1.- OPERATIONS.

    Yesterday evening the situation was normal, and remained so till 9.20 p.m., when a message was received from our Forward Battalion to say that the enemy was massing for opposite HOLLEBEKE from the direction of the CANAL. Our guns at once fired on their S.O.S. lines.

    The first intimation our forward posts had of any hostile intention was at 9.20 p.m., when parties of the enemy were seen crawling to our posts, and men were seen moving up in rear. Heavy Machine Gun and Rifle fire was turned on to them and our S.O.S. brought a thick and well timed barrage, which broke up the attack.

    At FORRET FARM too, he attacked and was held up by our Rifle and Machine Gun fire, and finally satisfactorily caught by our barrage.

    At 9.30 p.m. a message was received to say that our forward posts were still intact, and despite the encounter they remained so.

    The enemy put his barrage down along the outskirts of the Village, but owing to our posts having been pushed further out earlier in the day, we escaped many casualties.

    After this, things settled down to normal once more and our barrage was allowed to die down.

    The remainder of the night passed more quietly though at 3.15 a.m. the enemy put down a barrage between HOLLEBEKE and our original front line, this however did not materialise into any attack.

    We put down searching barrages at intervals along O 12 b, c and d and Machine guns kept the CANAL Bank under occasional bursts of fire.

    Apart from this, there was a heavy shelling of WHITE CHATEAU and the area in O 4 c with gas shells.

    OPAL RESERVE too received the same attention.

    The gas is described as having a slight irritating effect on the eyes and throat.

6-8-17.   Brigadier General.
                                          Commanding 122nd Infantry Brigade.

SECRET   B.M.141

Headquarters,
    41st Division. (G).

2

REPORT ON OPERATIONS OF JULY 31st 1917 & SUBSEQUENT DAYS.

Ref:- Map 28 S.W.5 A. WYTSCHAETE 1/10,000.

At 3.50 a.m. on 31st July 1917, the 122nd Infantry Brigade, in conjunction with the 56th Infantry Brigade (19th Division) on the Right, and the 123rd Infantry Brigade on the Left, attacked the enemy's position on a 1,200 yards front with two Battalions for the Assault, the 18th Bn. King's Royal Rifle Corps on the Right and the 11th Bn. Royal West Kent Regiment on the Left. The 12th Bn. East Surrey Regiment being in Support, and the 15th Bn. Hampshire Regiment in close Reserve.

The 122nd Machine Gun Company supported the attack, having a section with each of the Assaulting Battalions, a section behind OPTIC TRENCH to cover the front with direct fire in case of counter-attack, and a section in Reserve.

The 122nd Light Trench Mortar Battery supplied one Mortar to each of the four Battalions, two of them going over with the Assaulting Battalions.

OBJECTIVES.

The First Objective was the RED LINE which consisted of 150 yards of trench on the extreme right, certain enemy advanced positions in the centre, and a strongly held trench on the left (OBLIQUE TRENCH). (The latter was known to be strongly held as a reconnoitring patrol on the night 27/28th July was heavily bombed from it, and forced to retire).

The Second Objective, BLUE and GREEN LINES, included the village of HOLLEBEKE, known to be a nest of Machine Guns, and FORRET FARM another defended locality.

ASSEMBLY.

By 3.20 a.m. Battalions were ready in their Assembly positions. Tapes had been carefully laid out for Battalions to form up on, and these arrangements worked satisfactorily, but the 11th Bn. Royal West Kent Regiment, who had to assemble in NO MAN'S LAND, were observed and shelled, though little damage was done.

ZERO HOUR.

At 3.50 a.m. our barrage opened. It drew a ragged barrage from the enemy which fell about our Support area and the WHITE CHATEAU WOODS.

Attack/-

- 2 -

ATTACK

The waves pushed forward according to arrangement, satisfactorily.

The RED LINE was captured after a little delay on the left, due to the mist and wire, and considerable resistance at OBLIQUE TRENCH, and consolidation progressed about 150 yards in front.

The Second wave then pushed forward towards the BLUE LINE. Here progress was obstructed by a pocket of Machine Guns which were situated in the houses in O 6 c on the left, and by FORRET FARM on the right. One platoon under 2/Lt. PRESTON 11th Royal West Kent Regt. however, about 12 strong, managed to push forward along the outskirts of HOLLEBEKE and began digging in at O 12 a 3.4, it had, however, to fall back owing to its nearly being surrounded by the enemy.

At 5.15 a.m. 25 men were taken from the RED LINE, where consolidation was going on, and sent to re-inforce the right forward company, and at 7.49 a.m. as the position was still unsatisfactorily, Captain ROONEY 11th Royal West Kent Regiment and 50 men were sent from the left of the RED LINE to push forward and work through the Village. The party moved up under heavy sniping and machine gun fire, and after a tough fight with the enemy, at 11.30 a.m. reported that the village had been mopped up and that our front line was about 100 yards in rear of the GREEN LINE.

HOLLEBEKE held out for a long time, being stoutly defended by an Officer and about 20 men, the same party apparently, who had offered resistance earlier on, in the houses in O 6 c, and had by some means withdrawn into the village itself.

On the Right things were less satisfactorily, FORRET FARM still causing an obstruction. Subsequent events go to strengthen the assumption that the second wave after crossing the RED LINE, somehow lost direction, and went half left, thus becoming mixed up with the left battalion, leaving FORRET FARM on the right. They also, of course, lost their barrage and FORRET FARM remained uncleared.

Arrangements were made to Stokes Mortar the place at 11.30 a.m. At 11.55 a.m. however, a message was received saying that the Stokes Gun which was to bombard FORRET FARM, had been put out of action, so a company of the Right Battalion at the time engaged in consolidating the RED LINE, was ordered to go forward and rush the position.
Repeated messages were sent up to the company to this effect, but each time the runner was wounded, there being a heavy barrage down between our original front line and the WHITE CHATEAU WOODS; Captain BASSETT, M.C. 18th Bn. Kings Royal Rifle Corps was sent up to reconnoitre as to the exact situation, and if necessary, to command there, but he too was wounded and forced to return before ever reaching the company. It was then decided to organise a company of the 12th East Surrey Regiment (who after the assaulting battalions had left their trenches, came up and occupied them), to take FORRET FARM and withdraw the 18th Kings Royal Rifle Corps who had by this time suffered considerably and had lost their organisation.
It was subsequently found that a party of 8 men under Sergt. DIPLOCK 18th K.R.R. Corps, had reached their objective on the GREEN LINE south of the HOLLEBEKE Road.

Captain Howitt.

-3-

Captain HOWITT 12th Bn. East Surrey Regiment (since killed) with his company left the RED LINE at 7 p.m. on August 1st 1917, moved up behind the 11th Royal West Kent Regiment on the left, then swung to his right and took the houses on the road S.W. of HOLLEBEKE from the flank, captured them and took 8 more prisoners. A very neat little manouvre. He was assisted by Sergt. DIPLOCK 18th K.R.R.C. and the 6 men mentioned above, who remained 24 hours and did good work.

He extended his line to about 250 yards from FORRET FARM and thus the position remained for the night.

Touch was not got with the 19th Division on the Right, though endeavours were made to join them.

On the evening of the 2nd August two more platoons of the 12th East Surrey Regiment were sent up to fill the gaps, occupy front line, and get touch with 19th Division, which was successfully accomplished.

The line was thus established on approximately the GREEN LINE.

The enemy 10th Bavarians, were stout foes, and not the rabbits which Special Correspondents seem chiefly to hear of.

Prisoners taken were about 60, including 1 Officer. The identification was normal, being that of the 10th Bavarian Division, including the 8th and 16th R.I.R.

Our casualties, chiefly from machine guns were:-

	Killed.	Wounded.	Missing.
12th East Surrey Regt.	2 Offrs. 30 O.R.	1 Off. 102 O.R.	2 Offrs. 36 O.R.
15th Hampshire Regt.	1 Off. 14 O.R.	4 Offrs. 50 O.R.	1 Off. 2 O.R.
11th R.W. Kent Regt.	3 Offrs. 19 O.R.	7 Offrs. 182 O.R.	54 O.R.
18th K.R.R. Corps.	3 Offrs. 21 O.R.	3 Offrs. 88 O.R.	1 Off. 37 O.R.
122nd Machine Gun Coy.	1 Off. 6 O.R.	1 Off. 8 O.R.	1 Off. 1 O.R.
122nd Trench Mortar Batty.	3 O.R.	2 Off. 9 O.R.	

The enemy had shown great skill in the occupation of his positions, for though we had been in the line for several days, we had no idea whatever of his positions or strength, except OBLIQUE TRENCH.

Their snipers were very bold and active. Many of them were run over by our men in the dark and caused us many casualties.

BARRAGE.

Our barrage was good, but as usual with plain shrapnel, difficult to see. The smoke shells fired on the green line, were very effective, and were seen by all. Perhaps more smoke shells might be introduced into the Creeping barrage to mark positions.

R.E.

A part of 228th Field Company R.E. under 2/Lt. ADAIR, R.E. went forward at 7 a.m. and marked out a communication trench from OBLIQUE TRENCH forward to the BLUE LINE, and assisted in the wiring of the RED LINE.

TUNNELLERS/-

TUNNELLERS.

A Party of the 1st Canadian Tunnelling Company under Captain MAXWELL went over with the leading wave of the 11th Bn. Royal West Kent Regiment, for the purpose of examining dugouts and cellars to discover enemy mine charges if any.

WOUNDED.

Evacuation of wounded was a difficult matter while the weather was fine owing to the nature of the ground; when it rained it became most trying operations, but on the whole was successfully carried out.

Brigadier General.
Commanding 122nd Infantry Brigade.

6th August 1917.

REPORT ON THE OPERATIONS WHICH TOOK PLACE ON THE
MORNING OF THE 5th AUGUST.

At 4 a.m. on August 5th, in a heavy mist, the enemy attempted to retake HOLLEBEKE.

He succeeded in getting into FORRET FARM and then tried to take HOLLEBEKE, working round the village from the rear as well as from the front. On this occurring, Captain J.P.FOWLER slightly withdrew his Company from HOLLEBEKE and cut off a small party of Schturim Konfinde who had got behind him. The left, with the exception of one post of one officer and 15 men, held firm.

Very little information reaching Battalion Headquarters, Major G.D.AMERY and 2nd.Lieut.S.LASENBY went forward to clear up the situation. On further information, the two companies were sent forward to OPAL RESERVE. The Commanding Officer proceeded to OPTIC TRENCH. At that moment a message arrived from Captain J.P.FOWLER giving his dispositions. An immediate counter attack, under cover of the mist, was ordered. Major G.D.AMERY, having become a casualty, Captain C.C.OXBORROW's Company advanced with some men of the 12th East Surrey Regiment. One platoon from this reserve Company was detailed to attack FORRET FARM with the assistance of some men of the East Surrey Regiment. In addition, a Company was ordered to do the same thing, but came up on the East side of it.

The Village and FORRET FARM were cleared and 17 prisoners taken. In the meantime, while the above orders were being put into effect, by means of Major R.PENNELL's personally delivering the orders given, the Commanding Officer returned to the East Surrey Headquarters and asked for a slow rate of fire for a quarter of an hour, then rapid fire for the same period, followed again by a further period of slow fire. This was done and fortunately coincided with the attack on HOLLEBEKE.

On arrival of the platoon of the 15th Hampshire Regt. already referred to, near FORRET FARM a STAFFORD Officer was re-organising some of the EAST SURREY REGIMENT. He handed over command to 2nd.Lieut.P.E.SHIELDS and the HAMPSHIRES and SURREYS retook FORRET FARM taking 13 prisoners. A half company of the STAFFORDS were brought up at 2nd.Lieut. SHIELDS request and stood by in support, 200 yards in rear, but were not required.

They were however, good enough to escort some of the prisoners back.

(sd) C.D.V.CARY-BARNARD.
Lieut.Colonel.
8-8-17. Comdg.,15th Hampshire Regt.

SECRET   War Diary   Copy No. 2

122nd INFANTRY BRIGADE ORDER NO.131.

1.- On night 10th/11th August 15th Hampshire Regt. will be relieved in the Front Line by 11th Royal West Kent Regt. and 1 Company (3 Officers and 75 Other Ranks) 12th East Surrey Regiment.

2.- Front Line is at present held as shown on attached Plan. 11th Royal West Kent Regt. will take over from 'A', 'B' and 'C' Companies 15th Hampshire Regt., and 1 Company 12th East Surrey Regt. from 'D' Company 15th Hampshire Regt. This Company will then come under O.C.11th Royal West Kent Regt. for tactical purposes.
11th Royal West Kent Headquarters will take over Headquarters at O 5 c 5.9. from 15th Hampshire Regt.

3.- 15th Hampshire Regt. on relief will march by any route to DE ZON CAMP M 12 c 5.3.

4.- 12th East Surrey Regt. (Less 1 company) will move up as Support Battalion to OBLIQUE ROW, OPTIC TRENCH, OAK ROW and WHITE CHATEAU (Accommodation in latter for 50 men). Headquarters to BROKEN BRIDGE O4 b 2.4.
(Note:- WHITE CHATEAU is at present utilised by 15th Hampshire Regt. for resting 100 men, and will be equally shared by 11th R.W.Kent Regt. and 12th East Surrey Regt. Details of 12th East Surrey Regt. will not remain at DE ZON Camp, but will proceed to their transport Lines.

5.- The Platoons forming Composite Company under Captain POWLES, will rejoin their units on 10th August.
O.C.Composite Company will have his Company disposed as under by 6 p.m. 10th August.
Platoon of 12th East Surrey Regt.   in   OBLIQUE ROW.
Platoon of 11th R.W.Kent Regt.   in   WHITE CHATEAU.
Platoon of 18th K.R.R.Corps.   in   OAK RESERVES
Platoon of 15th Hampshire Regt. will be withdrawn by 15th Hampshire Regt. on relief.

6.- Transport arrangements and times of arrival of 12th East Surrey Regt. and 11th Royal West Kent Regt. in forward area will be issued later.

7.- Details of relief will be arranged between units concerned.

8.- ACKNOWLEDGE.

Issued at 11 p.m.
8th August 1917.

Captain.
Brigade Major.
122nd Infantry Brigade.

Copy No. 1 Filed.
No. 2 War Diary.
No. 3 41st Div.(G)
No. 4 41st Div.(Q).
No. 5 12th E.Surrey Regt.
No. 6 15th Hants Regt.
No. 7 11th R.W.Kent Regt.
No. 8 18th K.R.R.C.
No. 9 122nd M.G.Coy.
No.10 No.4 M.M.G.S.
No.11 122nd T.M.Battery.
No.12 123rd Inf.Bde.
No.13 124th Inf.Bde.
No.14 112th Inf.Bd.
No.15 228th Field Coy.
No.16 C.R.A.
No.17 Bde.Signals.
No.18 Staff Captain.

From:- Officer Commanding   K.E.16

            15th Hampshire Regt.

To:- Headquarters,

            122nd Infantry Brigade.

       With reference to this morning's operations these posts were advanced during the night to approximately O 11 b 9 2½., O 12 a 2.3., O 12 a 4.6.

       The three posts moved are those immediately in front of HOLLEBEKE as intended.

       The patrols which were to have been pushed forward under cover of this morning's barrage were not able to be sent out any distance owing to the fact that our barrage was very irregular in that some of the guns did not creep forward as they should have done.

Several guns were firing on the same line all the time, one or two behind my Posts.

       I would like to call attention to the fact that our artillery which two days ago was practically perfect has now, from some unknown cause, considerably deteriorated. One gun (reported to be six inch howitzer) on a magnetic bearing of 271° from FORRET FARM fires persistently short and yesterday wounded five of our own men. The line of this bearing runs through PHEASANT WOOD the south end of the DAMMSTRASSE.

Note.

       There is also a gap in our barrage between the left flank of the Division on our right and our right post at FORRET FARM.

                                      (sd) C.D.V.CARY-BARNARD,
                                                    Lieut.-Colonel.

10-8-17.   Commanding 15th Hampshire Regt.

SECRET   Copy No. 2

122nd INFANTRY BRIGADE ORDER No.132

Ref:- Map HAZEBROUCK 5A, 28 S.E. and 28 S.W.

1.- 122nd Infantry Brigade, less 122nd Machine Gun Company, will be relieved in the Right Sector by the 116th Infantry Brigade on the night 13th/14th August 1917, in accordance with the attached March Table.

2.- The 116th Infantry Brigade arrives at ELZENWALLE on the morning of 12th August.

3.- Details of relief will be arranged between Officers Commanding Units concerned.

4.- All Maps, plans, Defence Schemes, etc., will be handed over on relief.

5.- Completion of relief will be reported by code.

6.- 122nd Infantry Brigade Headquarters will close at I 33 d 1.. at 6 p.m. 13th inst., and re-open at ELZENWALLE at the same hour, at which time Command of the Right Sector will pass to G.O.C. 116th Infantry Brigade.

7.- Camps at ELZENWALLE will be allotted to units under arrangements to be made by Staff Captain direct with representatives of 12th East Surrey Regt., 11th Royal West Kent Regt., and 18th Kings Royal Rifle Corps respectively Details, who will provide guides where Overland Transport Track cuts ELZENWALLE - VIERSTRAAT Road H 36 c 4.2., to direct units into Camp.

8.- On 14th August the Brigade will move to FLETRE AREA. Details and Transport of all units and 122nd Trench Mortar Battery will move by March Route.
Remainder will embus at HALLEBAST CORNER between 10 and 11.30 a.m. on 14th inst. Accommodation in busses will be as under:-

      12th East Surrey Regt.   400.
      15th Hampshire Regt.   500.
      11th Royal West Kent Regt.   400.
      18th K.R.R.Corps.   400.
      122nd Machine Gun Coy.   70.

No baggage of any kind will be taken in busses, but lorries will be provided for surplus stores.
Detailed instructions for this move will follow later.

9.- ACKNOWLEDGE.

                                                            A.Y. Graham Thom
                                                                  Captain.
Issued at 1.30 p.m.   Brigade Major.
12th August 1917.   122nd Infantry Brigade.

Copy No. 1 Filed.   No.11 122nd T.M.Battery.
     No. 2 War Diary.   No.12 123rd Inf.Bde.
     No. 3 41st Division.   No.13 124th Inf.Bde.
     No. 4 12th E.Surrey Regt.   No.14 112th Inf.Bde.
     No. 5 15th Hants.Regt.   No.15 116th Inf.Bde.
     No. 6 11th R.W.Kent Regt.   No.16 228th Field Coy.
     No. 7 18th K.R.R.C.   No.17 C.R.A.
     No. 8 122nd M.G.Company.   No.18 Bde.Signals.
     No.10 No.4 M.M.G.S.   No.19 Bde.Transport Officer.
         No.20 No.2 Coy. Div.Train.
         21.138th Field Ambulance.
         22.Staff Captain.

MARCH TABLE TO ACCOMPANY 122nd INFANTRY BRIGADE ORDER No.122.

UNIT.	FROM	TO	RELIEVED BY	REMARKS.
11th Royal West Kent Regiment.	FRONT LINE	EIZENWALLE.	H.Q. 14th Hants.Regt. 2 Coys. 14th Hants.Regt. 2 Coys. 12th Royal Sussex.	Guides to be at OAK DUMP O 4 a 5.3. at 9 p.m.
12th East Surrey Regiment.	SUPPORT	-do-	H.Q.12th Royal Sussex Regt. 2 Coys.14th Hants.Regt. 2 Coys.Royal Sussex Regt.	Guides to be at OAK DUMP O 4 a 5.3. at 10 p.m.
18th Kings Royal Rifle Corps.	RESERVE.	-do-	11th Royal Sussex Regt.	Guides to be at junction of BUS HOUSE Road and WOODEN Road I 31 d 5.2. at 6 p.m.

SECRET War Diary   Copy No. 2

Reference 122nd INFANTRY BRIGADE ORDER No. 132.

Ref:- Map 27 S.E. 1/20,000 & Sketch attached.

1.- Billeting parties, strength as under, will report to the Brigade Transport Officer, at Brigade Transport Lines at N 7 & 6.7. at 9 a.m. tomorrow 13th August.

     Each Battalion..   1 Officer 5 N.C.Os.

     122nd Machine Gun Coy.   1 "   1 N.C.O.

     122nd Trench Mortar Batty. 1 Officer.

2.- Each member of the party will bring a bicycle, and rations for 14th inst.

3.- Party will proceed under senior officer present to the FLETRE Billeting Area and will report to Staff Captain 122nd Infantry Brigade at Brigade Headquarters X 1 d 2.2. at 12 noon.
Representatives from 228th Field Company R.E., No.2 Coy. A.S.C. and 139th Field Ambulance will also report to Staff Captain at the same hour.

4.- Billets are allotted to units as under:-

Unit	Location
Brigade Headquarters	X 1 d 2.2.
12th East Surrey Regt.	R 31 d 5.2.
15th Hampshire Regiment.	X 2 d 0.
11th Royal West Kent Regt.	X 2 c 8.2.
18th K.R.R.Corps.	X 1 d 5.1.
122nd Machine Gun Coy.	R 32 d 8.1.
122nd Trench Mortar Batty.	R 26 d 5.9.
228th Field Company R.E.	(R 32 c 2.3. (R 32 d 0.9.
No.2 Coy. A.S.C.	R 19 d 5.2.
139th Field Ambulance.	(X 2 b 3.2. (X 2 b 0.6. (R 32 d 9.5.

5.- ACKNOWLEDGE.

                           Captain.
                           Staff Captain.
12th August 1917.   122nd Infantry Brigade.

     Copy No. 1 Filed.
        No. 2 War Diary.
        No. 3 O.C. Details 12th E.Surrey Regt.
        No. 4 O.C. Details 11th R.W.Kent Regt.
        No. 5 O.C. Details 18th K.R.R.C.
        No. 6 O.C. Details 122nd M.G.Coy.
        No. 7 12th E.Surrey Regt.
        No. 8 15th Hants.Regt.
        No. 9 11th R.W.Kent Regt.
        No.10 18th K.R.R.C.
        No.11 122nd M.G.Coy.
        No.12 122nd T.M.Battery.
        No.13 228th Field Coy.R.E.
        No.14 No.2 Coy.A.S.C.
        No.15 139th Field Amb.
        No.16 Bde.Transport Officer.

SECRET   War Diary   Copy No.

122nd INFANTRY BRIGADE ORDER No.133.

Ref:- Map HAZEBROUCK 5A, 27 S.E. and 28 S.W.

1.- No.4 Battery Motor M.G.S. and 122nd Machine Gun Company will be relieved by 116th Machine Gun Company in the line on night 12th/13th August.
Details will be arranged between D.M.G.Os and Commanders concerned.
Completion of relief will be reported to this office by the phrase 'Limber up'.

2.- No.4 Battery M.M.G.S. will return to its normal camp on relief.
Personnel of 122nd Machine Gun Company will rejoin remainder of the Company.

3.- On 13th August 122nd Machine Gun Company will move to FLETRE AREA, and will occupy billet at R 33 a 2.3. (previously occupied by 228th Field Company R.E.)
Instructions for billetting party for new area will be issued later.

4.- Personnel to the number of 70 will embus at HALLEBAST CORNER at 5.05 p.m. on 13th August to proceed to new area.
Transport and details will move from waggon lines by March Route via WESTOUTRE and BERTHEN on afternoon of 13th August under orders to be issued by O.C. 122nd Machine Gun Company.

5.- No baggage will be taken on busses.
Surplus stores will be dumped and left under a guard at waggon lines, to be brought on by lorry shared with 122nd Trench Mortar Battery.

6.- Rations will be drawn on 13th August as usual for consumption on 14th inst. Rations for consumption on 15th August will be issued from dump in new area.

7.- ACKNOWLEDGE.

                                       signature
                                       Captain.
                                       Brigade Major.
Issued at 1.30 p.m.   122nd Infantry Brigade.
12th August 1917.

           Copy No.1 Filed.
              No. 2 War Diary.
              No. 3 41st Division.
              No. 4 12th E.Surrey Regt.
              No. 5 15th Hants.Regt.
              No. 6 11th R.W.Kent Regt.
              No. 7 18th K.R.R.C.
              No. 8 122nd M.G.Coy.
              No. 9 No.4 Bty.M.M.G.S.
              No.10 122nd T.M.Batty.
              No.11 123rd Inf.Bde.
              No.12 124th Inf.Bde.
              No.13 112th Inf.Bde.
              No.14 116th Inf.Bde.
              No.15 No.2 Coy.Train.
              No.16 228th Field Coy.
              No.17 138th Field Amb.
              No.18 Bde.Signals.
              No.19 Bde.Transport Officer.
              No.20 Staff Captain.
              No.21 C.R.A.

SECRET  Copy No.....

AMENDMENT TO 122nd INFANTRY BRIGADE ORDER No.132.

1.- Reference 122nd Infantry Brigade Order No.132, para.6. 122nd Infantry Brigade Headquarters will close at I 33 d 1.6. at 6 p.m. on 13th August 1917, and reopen at ELZENWALLE at same hour. Command of the Right Sector will pass to G.O.C. 116th Infantry Brigade on completion of relief, up to which time an Advanced Report Centre will be kept open at I 33 d 1.6.

2.- ACKNOWLEDGE.

Captain.
Brigade Major.
122nd Infantry Brigade.

12th August 1917.

To all recipients of O.O. 132.

S E C R E T   War Diary   Copy No. 2...

122nd INFANTRY BRIGADE ORDER No. 134.

Ref:- Maps HAZEBROUCK 5A, 27 S.E. and 28 S.W.

1.- 122nd Infantry Brigade less 122nd Machine Gun Company will move to the FLETRE Area (plan attached) on 14th August.

2.- Units will march to place of embussing, and embus in accordance with Table attached, following the instructions detailed below.

    (a) Maximum accommodation in each Bus 25 all ranks, exclusive of the driver and mate.

    (b) Busses will be drawn up on right hand side of the road 15 yards to each bus.

    (c) Troops will be in position on left of road in parties of 25 to each 15 yards, ten minutes before scheduled time of departure of convoy.

    (d) Embussing will only commence on receipt of orders from Divisional Staff Officer in charge.

    (e) Captain G.W. HOWARD 18th Kings Royal Rifle Corps will act as Staff Officer 122nd Infantry Brigade.

    (f) No baggage of any kind may be taken in the busses.

3.- Details and transport of units and 122nd Trench Mortar battery will proceed by march route to new area via WESTOUTRE and BERTHEN as under:-

UNIT.	FROM.	TO.	Time of dep.
18th K.R.R.C. Transport & Details less Cookers & Water carts.	Transport Lines N 7 a 6.8.	X 1 d 5.1.	10 a.m.
15th Hants.Regt. Transport & Details.	-do-	X 2 d 0.4.	10.10 a.
12th E.Surrey Regt. Transport & Details. Less cookers & W.Carts.	-do-	R 31 d 4.1.	10.20 a.
11th R.W.Kent Regt. Transport & Details. Less Cookers & W.Carts.	-do-	X 2 c 2.2.	10.30 a.
122nd T.M.Battery.	WOOD CAMP M 5 d 5.5.	R 26 d 5.0.	9.0 a.m.
Bde.H.Q. Transport. and Cookers, W.Carts, & Mess Carts as required.	ELZENWALLE.) 12th E.Surreys.) of 11th R.W.Kents.) 18th K.R.R.C.	X 1 d 2.2. Respective billets.	8.30 a.

4.- Baggage wagons will report to units at 5 p.m. 13th August, and will accompany either Transport from Transport Lines, or from ELZENWALLE as required by units.

5.- Information about Lorries will be issued later.

6.- Rations for 15th August will be drawn on 14th August on arrival in new area.

7.- 140 Field Amb./9

- 2 -

7.- 140th Field Ambulance will move to FLETRE AREA W 5 c 3.9. on night 14th/15th and receive Sick of 122nd Infantry Brigade Group from 15th inst. inclusive.

8.- Staff Captain will meet billetting parties as already detailed at New Brigade Headquarters X 1 d 2.2. 12 noon 13th August.

9.- Brigade Headquarters will close at ELZENWALLE at 9.30 a.m. 14th August and re-open at ROUKOSHILLE X 1.d 3.2. at the same hour.

10.- ACKNOWLEDGE.

Issued at 7.30 a.m.
13th August 1917.

Captain.
Brigade Major.
122nd Infantry Brigade.

Copy No. 1 Filed.
No. 2 War Diary.
No. 3 41st Division.
No. 4 12th E.Surrey Regt.
No. 5 15th Hampshire Regt.
No. 6 11th R.W.Kent Regt.
No. 7 18th K.R.R.Corps.
No. 8 122nd M.G.Company.
No. 9 122nd T.M.Battery.
No.10 O.C.Details 12th E.Surreys.
No.11 O.C.Details 11th R.W.Kents.
No.12 O.C.Details 18th K.R.R.C.
No.13 123rd Inf.Bde.
No.14 124th Inf.Bde.
No.15 112th Inf.Bde.
No.16 116th Inf.Bde.
No.17 228th Field Coy.R.E.
No.18 140th Field Amb.
No.19 No.2 Coy.Train.
No.20 Staff Captain.
No.21 Bde.Transport Officer.
No.22 Bde.Signal Section.

MARCH and EMBUSSING TABLE.

UNIT.	FROM	TO	ROUTE	REMARKS.
18th K.R.R.Corps. (Not to exceed 400 all ranks).	Camp ELZENWALLE.	Place of Embussing N 2 b 65.60. (On main HALLEBAST - LA CLYTTE Road, 200 yards South of HALLEBAST Cross Roads.	An officer from Details of Units will reconnoitre route leaving the HALLEBAST CORNER-VIERSTRAAT Road clear for troops of 39th Division. He will report to O.C.of his Unit in ELZENWALLE CAMP with information as to Route and length of time march will take.	To embus in Convoy 'A'. Leaving at 10.0 a.m.
12th East Surrey Regt. (Not to exceed 400 all ranks).	-do-	-do-	-do-	To embus in Convoy 'C'. Leaving at 11 a.m.
11th R.W.Kent Regt. (Not to exceed 400 all ranks).	-do-	-do-	-do-	To embus in Convoy 'D'. Leaving at 11.30 a.m.
15th Hampshire Regt. (Not to exceed 500 all ranks).	MURRUMBIDGEE CAMP.	-do-	To march under orders of O.C. Unit.	To embus in Convoy 'B'. Leaving at 10.30 a.m.

12th East Surrey Regt.
15th Hampshire Regt.
11th Royal West Kent Regt.
18th Kings Royal Rifle Corps.
122nd Machine Gun Company.
122nd Trench Mortar Battery.
Brigade Signal Section.
228th Field Company R.E.
41st Division (G).   )
123rd Infantry Brigade.) For information.

B.M.337

1.- The Army Commander is inspecting the 122nd Infantry Brigade and the 228th Field Company R.E. (All units less transport) on Saturday 18th August at 11.50 a.m. on Football Ground at X 14 b 6.5. near METEREN.

2.- Dress - Drill Order - belts and side arms without pouches or braces. P.H. Helmets to be worn.

3.- The Brigade and 228th Field Company R.E. will be drawn up as described in B.M.316 for Divisional Commander's Inspection.

4.- Bayonets will be fixed and Officers will take post in Review Order.

5.- The Army Commander will be received with a General Salute. Massed Bands of the 11th Royal West Kent Regiment and 18th Kings Royal Rifle Corps will play the Salute but will not play during the Inspection.

6.- Units will march to the place of Parade in accordance with the attached Table.

7.- Right Markers will report to an Officer of the Brigade Staff on the Ground at 10.40 a.m.

8.- Parade will be as strong as possible.
Parade States of Units will be rendered to this office by 6 p.m. 17th August, showing Total Strength, Ration Strength, and Parade Strength.

9.- ACKNOWLEDGE.

16th August 1917.

Captain.
Brigade Major.
122nd Infantry Brigade.

MARCH TABLE.

UNIT.	STARTING POINT.	Time Head to pass Starting Point.	ROUTE	REMARKS.
18th Kings Royal Rifle Corps.	Shrine X 1 d 6.1.	10.22 a.m.	Via X 14 b 2.3.	Route via X 9 c 9.5, to be left clear for 123rd Inf.Brigade.
11th Royal West Kent Regt.	-do-	10.28 a.m.	-do-	-do-
15th Hampshire Regiment.	-do-	10.34 a.m.	-do-	-do-
12th East Surrey Regiment.	-do-	10.40 a.m.	-do-	-do-
228th Field Company R.E.	-do-	10.45 a.m.	-do-	-do-
122nd Machine Gun Company.	-do-	10.47 a.m.	-do-	-do-
122nd Trench Mortar Battery.	-do-	10.49 a.m.	-do-	-do-
Brigade Signal Section.	-do-	10.50 a.m.	-do-	-do-

12th East Surrey Regt.
15th Hampshire Regt.
11th Royal West Kent Regt.
18th Kings Royal Rifle Corps.
122nd Machine Gun Company.
122nd Trench Mortar Battery.
Brigade Signal Section.
228th Field Company R.E.
   41st Division (G).)
123rd Infantry Brigade.) For information.

B.M.337

1.- The Army Commander is inspecting the 122nd Infantry Brigade and the 228th Field Company R.E. (All units less transport) on Saturday 18th August at 11.50 a.m. on Football Ground at X 14 b 6.5. near METEREN.

2.- Dress - Drill Order - belts and side arms without pouches or braces.   P.H. Helmets to be worn.

3.- The Brigade and 228th Field Company R.E. will be drawn up as described in B.M.316 for Divisional Commander's Inspection.

4.- Bayonets will be fixed and Officers will take post in Review Order.

5.- The Army Commander will be received with a General Salute. Massed Bands of the 11th Royal West Kent Regiment and 18th Kings Royal Rifle Corps will play the Salute but will not play during the Inspection.

6.- Units will march to the place of Parade in accordance with the attached Table.

7.- Right Markers will report to an Officer of the Brigade Staff on the Ground at 10.40 a.m.

8.- Parade will be as strong as possible.
    Parade States of Units will be rendered to this office by 6 p.m. 17th August, showing Total Strength, Ration Strength, and Parade Strength.

9.- ACKNOWLEDGE.

16th August 1917.

                                   Captain.
                              Brigade Major.
                      122nd Infantry Brigade.

MARCH TABLE.

UNIT.	STARTING POINT.	Time Head to pass Starting Point.	ROUTE	REMARKS.
16th Kings Royal Rifle Corps.	Spring X 1 d 6.1.	10.22 a.m.	Via X 14 b 2.3.	Route via X 9 c 9.6. to be left clear for 123rd Inf.Brigade.
11th Royal West Kent Regt.	-do-	10.28 a.m.	-do-	-do-
15th Hampshire Regiment.	-do-	10.34 a.m.	-do-	-do-
13th East Surrey Regiment.	-do-	10.40 a.m.	-do-	-do-
228th Field Company R.E.	-do-	10.45 a.m.	-do-	-do-
122nd Machine Gun Company.	-do-	10.47 a.m.	-do-	-do-
122nd Trench Mortar Battery.	-do-	10.49 a.m.	-do-	-do-
Brigade Signal Section.	-do-	10.50 a.m.	-do-	-do-

12th East Surrey Regt.
15th Hampshire Regt.
11th Royal West Kent Regt.
18th Kings Royal Rifle Corps.
122nd Machine Gun Company.
122nd Trench Mortar Battery.
Brigade Signal Section.
228th Field Company.
41st Division.   )
123rd Infantry Brigade.) For information.

B.M.316

1.- The Divisional Commander is inspecting 122nd Infantry Brigade and 228th Field Company R.E. (All units without transport) on the Football Field at X 14 b 9.5. by side of main METEREN - FLETRE Road at 11 a.m. on Friday 17th August 1917.

2.- Dress - Fighting Order with F.S. Dress Caps and P.H.G. Helmets (No box respirators).

3.- Units will move to the Parade Ground in accordance with the attached Table and be formed up by 10.45 a.m. on three sides of a square as per plan below.
228th Field Company R.E. will be in close column of sections with attached Platoons in close column of Platoons.
Battalions in close column of companies.
122nd Machine Gun Company in close column of sections.
122nd Trench Mortar Battery in close column of two sections, each section being composed of 4 teams.
The 122nd Brigade Signal Section will be formed up in two ranks.

```
              15th Hants Regt.    11th R.W.Kent Regt.
              ┌──────────────────────────────────────┐
12th E.Surrey ┤                                      ├ 18th K.R.R.C.
Regt.         │                                      │
Att.Platoons. ┤                                      ├ 122nd M.G.Coy.
              │                                      │
228th Field   ┤                                      ├ 122nd T.M.B.
Company R.E.  │                                      │
              │                                      ├ Bde.Sig.Sect.
```

4.- Frontages are allotted as follows:-
   228th Field Company R.E.   15 yards.
   Att.Platoons.   15 "
   12th E.Surrey Regiment.   60 "
   15th Hampshire Regiment.   60 "
   11th R.W.Kent Regiment.   40 "
   18th K.R.R.Corps.   60 "
   122nd Machine Gun Coy.   15 "
   122nd Trench Mortar Batty.   15 "
   Brigade Signal Section.   15 "

5.- Right Markers of all units will report to an officer of the Brigade Staff on the ground at 10.0 a.m. 17th inst.

6.- Bands of the 11th R.W.Kent Regt. and 18th K.R.R.Corps will be on parade.

7.- ACKNOWLEDGE.

Captain.
Brigade Major.
122nd Infantry Brigade.

16th Aug 1917.

MARCH TABLE.

UNIT.	STARTING POINT	Time Head to pass Starting Point.	ROUTE	REMARKS.
10th K.R.R.Corps.	SHRINE X 1 d 6.1.	9.50 a.m.	Via X 14 b 2.9.	
11th R.W.Kent Regt.	-do-	9.55 a.m.	-do-	
12th E.Surrey Regt.	-do-	10.0 a.m.	-do-	
Bde.Signal Section.	-do-	10.05 a.m.	-do-	
15th Hampshire Regt.	Road Junction X 3 c 1.4.	9.50 a.m.	Via X 9 c 9.6.	
228th Field Coy.R.E.	-do-	9.56 a.m.	-do-	
122nd Machine Gun Coy.	-do-	9.58 a.m.	-do-	
122nd Trench Mortar Battery.	-do-	10.0 a.m.	-do-	

122nd INFANTRY BRIGADE.

PARADE STATE.

for ARMY COMMANDER'S INSPECTION, 18th AUGUST 1917.

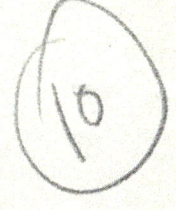

UNIT.	TOTAL STRENGTH.		RATION STRENGTH.		PARADE STRENGTH.	
	Officers.	O.R's.	Officers.	O.R's.	Officers.	O.R's.
12th E.Surrey Regt.	38.	688.	21.	575.	18.	425.
15th Hampshire Regt.	33.	878.	23.	630.	20.	482.
11th R.W.Kent Regt.	25.	609.	17.	452.	14.	312.
18th K.R.R.Corps.	35.	810.	26.	664.	24.	527.
122nd M.Gun Coy.	11.	147.	10.	133.	8.	280.
122nd T.M.Bty.	4.	72.	2.	56.	1.	60.
122nd Bde.Sig.Sect.	1.	40.	1.	40.	1.	23.
228th Field Coy.R.E.	7.	203.	5.	181.	5.	132.
Attached:-						
12th E.Surreys.	-	26.	-	26.	-	18.
15th Hants.	-	36.	-	34.	-	30.
11th Kents.	1.	30.	1.	28.	1.	22.
18th K.R.R.C.	1.	26.	1.	26.	1.	21.
TOTAL,	x 154.	3447.	107.	2845.	93.	2132.

N.B. x-Total Strength does not include the personnel attached to the 228th Field Company., R.E.

18.8.17

F W Towsey
B.G.C.
122nd Inf Bde

"A" Form.
MESSAGES AND SIGNALS.

Army Form C. 2121 (in pads of 100).
No of Message **36**

Prefix	Code	m	Words	Charge	This message is on a/c of:	Recd. at	m.
Office of Origin and Service Instructions.			Sent		Service	Date	
			At ... m.			From	
			To				
			By		(Signature of "Franking Officer.")	By	

TO ~~DAGGER~~ ~~LOYALTY~~
~~HAMLET~~ THEORIST
~~ROXY~~ ~~(GOLD)~~

| Sender's Number. | Day of Month. | In reply to Number. | AAA |
| BM 346 | 19 | | |

Ref Addendum to OD 135 aaa for T10B0.9 please read T10B8.9.

From **BELL**
Place
Time **10/5 pm**

The above may be forwarded as now corrected. (Z)

Censor. Signature of Addressor or person authorised to telegraph in his name
* This line should be erased if not required.

SECRET

ADDEMDUM

to

122nd INFANTRY BRIGADE ORDER No. 135.

War Diary

1.- Brigade Headquarters will close at X 1 d 2.2. at 6.30 a.m. 20
and re-open at LE NIEPPE T 10 b 0.9. at the same hour.

2.- Units will issue written instructions to lorry drivers
to proceed to STAPLE CHURCH, to await instructions from
units at this point.

                                                Captain.
                                            Brigade Major.
19-8-17.   122nd Infantry Brigade.

To all recipients of 122nd Inf.Bde. O.O. No.135.

SECRET   Copy No. 2

122nd INFANTRY BRIGADE ORDER No. 135.

Ref:- Map Sheet 27 1/40,000 & HAZEBROUCK 5A 1/100,000.

1.- 122nd Infantry Brigade Group will march to the EBBLINGHEM Area on August 20th in accordance with the attached Table.

2.- Normal halts after 6 a.m. will be observed throughout the march.
Intervals of 100 yards between Units, and 50 yards between Infantry Companies will be maintained.

3.- Guides to Billets will meet all units on their arrival at STAPLE CHURCH.

4.- Transport and Baggage waggons will accompany Units.

5.- Lorries will be allotted as follows:-

    Brigade Headquarters
    Each Battalion   3 except 11th Bn.Royal
    West Kent Regt.   2 only.
    228th Field Company R.E.   1
    Machine Gun Company   )
    Trench Mortar Battery.   )   1 together.

1 Guide per lorry from units will meet lorries at 6 a.m. on August 20th at Road junction X 3 c 05.45.

6.- Rations for consumption on 20th inst. will be carried on the man and 1st Line Transport.
Units will report their arrival in Camp by runner to Brigade Headquarters at LE NIEPPE T 10 b 8.9.
These Runners will be utilised to guide Supply lorries to their units with rations for consumption on 21st August.

7.- 140th Field Ambulance will, on arrival, send two Ambulances to Brigade Headquarters, where they will be notified of positions of units, and will then proceed round units to collect Sick.

8.- All tents and shelters, and area stores, will be left in the present area.
Certificates from Commanding Officers that Areas have been left in a clean condition will be forwarded to this office.

9.- March will be resumed to the BOISDENGHEM - ACQUIN and WESTRECOURT Area on the 21st inst. under orders to be issued later. Busses will be provided to assist Transport of personnel, and will leave LE NIEPPE between 8 and 9 a.m. on 21st inst.
Battalions may calculate on being able to embus all ranks up to a number of 400 each.
Field Company and attached Platoons to the number of 250.
122nd Machine Gun Company and 122nd Trench Mortar Battery 100.
122nd Brigade Headquarters 50.
Lorries will be available as for move on 20th inst.

10.- ACKNOWLEDGE.

                                              Captain.
Issued to Sigs at 7.30 p.m.   Brigade Major.
19th August 1917.   122nd Infantry Brigade.

Copy No. 1 Filed.   No. 7 18th K.R.R.C.   No. 13
    No. 2 War Diary.   No. 8 122nd M.G.Coy.   No. 14 122nd I.Bde.
    No. 3 41st Div.'G'   No. 9 122nd T.M.B.   No. 15
    No. 4 12th E.Surreys   No.10 228th Field Co.   No. 16
    No. 5 15th Hants.   No.11 140th Fld.Amb.   No. 17 Staff Capt.
    No. 6 11th R.W.K.   No.12 No.2 Coy.Train.

MARCH TABLE to accompany 122nd INFANTRY BRIGADE ORDER No.135

UNIT.	FROM	TO	S.P.	Time Head to pass S.P.	ROUTE	REMARKS.
2th East Surrey Regt.	R 31 d 4.2.	EBBLINGHEM - LE NIEPPE - ZUYTPEENE. Area.	Cross Roads LE ROUKLOSHILLE K 1 a 8.9.	5.48 a.m.	FLETRE - CAESTRE - HONDEGHEM Station.	Whole column to be clear of FLETRE by 7 a.m. (123rd Inf. Bde.Group follow on same road from FLETRE at 7.30 a.m.)
8th Kings Royal Rifle Corps.	X 1 d 5.2.	-do-	-do-	5.58 a.m.	-do-	
11th Royal West Kent Regiment.	X 2 c 2.2.	-do-	-do-	6.00 a.m.	-do-	
15th Hampshire Regiment.	X 2 d 1.4.	-do-	-do-	6.18 a.m.	-do-	
Brigade Headquarters.	X 1 d 2.2.	T 10 b 3.9.	-do-	6.28 a.m.	-do-	
228th Field Coy. R.E.	R 33 a 2.4.		-do-	6.29 a.m.	-do-	
122nd Machine Gun Coy.	R 32 d 8.1.		-do-	6.35 a.m.	-do-	
122 Trench Mortar Batty.	R 26 d 0.5.	Near LES TROIS ROIS O 26 b 3.9.	-do-	6.40 a.m.	-do-	
No.2 Coy.Divnl.Train.	R 19 d 5.2.		-do-	6.42 a.m.	-do-	
40th Field Ambulance. (Less 1 Section).	W 5 c 3.9.		Road junction W 4 d 8.6.	7.10 a.m.	-do-	

SECRET.   Copy No..2...

122nd INFANTRY BRIGADE ORDER No.136.

Ref:- Map Sheet 27 1/40,000 & HAZEBROUCK 5A 1/100,000.

1.- 122nd Infantry Brigade Group (less 228th Field Company R.E.) will move by route to the BOISDINGHEM AREA on 21st August 1917.
228th Field Company R.E. will move under orders of 123rd Infantry Brigade.

2.- Personnel will embus in accordance with the attached BUS Table.
Busses will arrive in three convoys and halt on right hand side of the road with 15 yards between each bus.
Head of convoy in each case will halt at Cross Roads LE NIEPPE.
Units will divide their personnel into parties of 25 all ranks.
These parties will be drawn up a quarter of an hour before the scheduled time of arrival of busses, on the left hand side of the road in order named in the Table, at 15 yards interval between parties, leading party at Cross roads LE NIEPPE. Not more than 25 of all ranks will embark on one bus, and no kits will be carried.
Troops will embus under direction of an officer of Brigade Staff.

3.- Details and Transport of Units, 122nd Trench Mortar Battery, No.2 Company Train and 140th Field Ambulance will march in accordance with the attached Table. Normal halts will be observed. There will be an hour halt on route for watering and feeding, to be arranged by the Brigade Transport Officer.

4.- Billeting Parties will rendezvous at LE NIEPPE CHURCH at 3.30 p.m. to-day.

5.- Lorries as previously detailed will park with Units to-night and proceed under orders of C.O's of Units concerned on 21st inst. O.C. 140th Field Ambulance will share lorry allotted to 228th Field Company R.E. who are billeting at SETQUES.
On completion of journey all lorries will be sent to Brigade Headquarters at BOISDINGHEM, where a convoy will be formed preparatory to their return to their column.

6.- Railhead for 122nd Infantry Brigade changes from BAILLEUL to ST OMER on 21st instant.
Rations for consumption on 22nd inst. will be issued on 21st inst. in new area. Units will send guides to rendezvous at Road junction E. end of WIZEANES at 3 p.m. 21st inst.
Supply Officer will explain to representatives of units system of supply after 21st August.

7.- O.C. 140th Field Ambulance will detail 2 Ambulances to visit all Battalion Headquarters as soon after 6 a.m. 21st inst. as possible, to pick up sick. Other units will send their sick to the nearest Battalion Headquarters.

8.- Brigade Headquarters will close at LE NIEPPE at 10 a.m. 21st inst. and re-open at BOISDINGHEM at the same hour.

9.- ACKNOWLEDGE.

Issued at 1.30 p.m.
20th August 1917.

Captain.
Brigade Major,
122nd Infantry Brigade.

Copy No. 1. Filed.
     No. 2 War Diary.
     No. 3 41st Div. 'G'.
     No. 4 12th E.Surreys.
     No. 5 11th R.W.K.
     No. 6 15th Hants.
     No. 7 18th K.R.R.C.
     No. 8 122nd M.G.Coy.
     No. 9 122nd T.M.Bty.
     No.10 228th Field Coy.
     No.11 140th Field Ambulance.
     No.12 No.2 Coy Train.
     No.13 123rd Inf. Bde.
     No.14 124th Inf. Bde.
     No.15 Bde. Signal Section.
     No.16 Brigade T.O.
     No.17 Staff Captain.

MARCH TABLE.

UNIT	FROM	TO	STARTING POINT	Time Head to pass S.P.	ROUTE	REMARKS.
Transport & Details 18th K.R.R.Corps.	LE NIEPPE	WESTBECOURT	Cross Roads LE NIEPPE.	9.15 a.m.	ARQUES - ST.OMER - ST.MARTIN.	To be clear of ARQUES by 11 a.m. After ST.MARTIN units will take nearest route to their billetting area.
Transport & Details 15th Hampshire Regt.	EBBLINGHEM	ACQUIN Area.	-do-	9.17 a.m.	-do-	
Brigade Headquarters.	LE NIEPPE.	BOISINGHEM	-do-	9.19 a.m.	-do-	
Transport & Details 11th R.W.Kent Regt.	LES TROIS ROIS	BOISINGHEM	-do-	9.20 a.m.	-do-	
Transport & Details 122nd Machine Gun Coy.	-do-	ZUTOVE.	-do-	9.22 a.m.	-do-	
No.2 Coy.Train.	-do-	ACQUIN Area	-do-	9.24 a.m.	-do-	
Transport & Details 12th East Surrey Regt.	ZUYTPEENE.	ZUDAUSQUES Area	-do-	9.26 a.m.	-do-	
2nd Trench Mortar Batty.	LES TROIS ROIS	ZUDAUSQUES Area	-do-	9.28 a.m.	-do-	
140th Field Ambulance.	-do-	WATTINE.	-do-	9.29 a.m.	-do-	

E J S   T A B L E.

Time of arrival of bus.	CONVOY No.	No. of Busses.	Total Number all ranks.	All Ranks of UNITS.		TO.
8 a.m.	1	26	650	18th K.R.R.Corps.	500	WESTBECOURT.
				15th Hampshire Regt.	150	ACQUIN.
8.30 a.m.	2	26	650	15th Hampshire Regt.	350	ACQUIN.
				11th R.W.Kent Regt.	300	BOISDINGHEM.
9 a.m.	3	26	650	11th R.W.Kent Regt.	100	BOISDINGHEM.
				Brigade Headquarters.	50	BOISDINGHEM.
				122nd Machine Gun Co.	90	ZUTOWE.
				122nd T.M.Battery.	10	ZUTOWE (To await guides)
				12th East Surrey Regt.	400	ZUDAUSQUES.

Vol 15

Headquarters,
122nd Inf. Bde.
(1st X(a))
July 1917

(6339) Wt. W160/M3016 1,500,000 10/17 McA & W Ltd (E1898) Forms W3091. Army Form W.3091.

Cover for Documents.

Nature of Enclosures.

~~OPERATION ORDERS~~

****

~~44th Infantry Brigade~~

Notes, or Letters written.

SECRET

Headquarters,   B.G.316
    41st Division. (Q).A

    Herewith War Diaries of Headquarters and Units of
the 122nd Infantry Brigade for the month of JULY, with
the exception of 11th Royal West Kent Regt, which will
follow as soon as received.

                                                       Brigadier General.
                          Commanding 122nd Infantry Brigade.

2-8-17.

Army Form C. 2118

WAR DIARY
or
INTELLIGENCE SUMMARY
(Erase heading not required.)

Instructions regarding War Diaries and Intelligence Summaries are contained in F.S. Regs., Part II. and the Staff Manual respectively. Title Pages will be prepared in manuscript.

Place	Date	Hour	Summary of Events and Information	Remarks and references to Appendices
LA ROUKLOSHILLE AREA.	JULY 1917.		122nd INFANTRY BRIGADE.	
	1st		Brigadier General F.W.TOWSEY C.M.G. returns from leave and re-assumes Command of the Brigade, vice Lt.-Col.A.C.CORFE D.S.O, 11th Royal West Kent Regt. who acted in his absence. Captain G.D.AINGER M.C. also returned from leave.	
	2nd		Training.	
	3rd		The Brigade Major, Captain A.Y.GRAHAM THOMSON M.C. and Lt.-Col.A.C.CORFE 11th Royal West Kent Regt. proceeded on leave. Lieut.F.G.BUCHANAN (Signalling Officer) returns from leave.	
	4th		Lieut.F.G.BUCHANAN proceeds to 39th Division Headquarters to take up duties of Signalling Officer R.A.	
	5th) 6th) 7th)		Training.	
	8th		Church Parade was held.	
	9th 10th			
	11th		Lieut.REAH (Intelligence Officer) proceeds on leave. Training and re-organising continues. Brigade O.O.No.125 issued. Draft of 1 Officer and 60 O.R. for 18th Kings Royal Rifle Corps.	App.1
	12th		Bombing, Re-organising and Training.	
	13th		Major General S.T.B.LAWFORD, C.B. Commanding 41st Division inspects the 122nd Infantry Brigade and had lunch at Brigade Headquarters. Honours and Awards won presented to recipients of each unit.	
	14th		The Brigade Major, Captain A.Y.GRAHAM THOMSON, M.C. returns from leave and re-assumes his duties vice Captain G.D.AINGER, M.C. who acted in his absence. Brig.-General F.W.TOWSEY, C.M.G. went to Divisional Garden Party at BERTHEN.	

WAR DIARY or INTELLIGENCE SUMMARY

(Erase heading not required.)

Army Form C. 2118

122nd Infantry Brigade.

Place	Date	Hour	Summary of Events and Information	Remarks and references to Appendices
JULY 1917 LA KREUKLOSHILLE AREA.	15th) 16th) 17th)		Training and re-organising carried out in Military areas.	
	18th		122nd Brigade Order No.127 issued with Administrative Arrangements re same. Training etc. in Billets.	App.2.
	19th		In Billets. Training and re-organising.	" 3
	20th		Practice attack carried out on Training area at R 18 a, fairly successful. Further Administrative arrangements to O.O.127 issued.	" 4
	21st		122nd Infantry Brigade Order No.128 issued.	
	22nd.		Brigade Instructions Nos. 1, 3 and 8 issued ref.O.O.127, and amendments issued.	" 5&6
WESTOUTRE	23rd		Brigade moves into WESTOUTRE AREA as per Brigade Order No.128. Report Centre at X 1 d.2.2. closes at 9.30 a.m. and opens at M 10 d 8.7. at same hour. Brigade Order No.129 issued.	" 7
	24th		122nd Infantry Brigade relieves 140th Infantry Brigade in the line in Sub-Sector South of CANAL. Brigade Headquarters closes at M 10 & 7.6. at 6 p.m. and opens at SPOIL BANK at same hour when Command passes. Brigade Instructions No.2 ref.O.O.127 issued.	" 8
	25th		Casualties - 12th E.Surrey Regt. 1 O.R.Wounded. 15th Hampshire Regt. 7 O.R.Wounded. 11th R.W.Kent Regt. 1 Officer Killed 14 O.R.Wounded. 18th K.R.R.Corps. 2 O.R.Wounded. 122nd Machine Gun Coy. 1 O.R.Wounded.	
	26th		Quiet day. Practice Barrage put down at 5 p.m. Brigadier General SKINNER,D.S.O. G.O.C.41st Infantry Brigade visited Brigade Headquarters preparatory to his Brigade taking over the line at a later date.	

Army Form C. 2118

WAR DIARY
or
INTELLIGENCE SUMMARY
(Erase heading not required.)

Instructions regarding War Diaries and Intelligence Summaries are contained in F. S. Regs., Part II. and the Staff Manual respectively. Title Pages will be prepared in manuscript.

Place: 122nd Infantry Brigade
JULY 1917

Date	Hour	Summary of Events and Information	Remarks and references to Appendices
26th		Casualties - 12th East Surrey Regt. 5 O.R.Wounded. 15th Hants.Regt. 1 O.R.Wounded. 11th R.W.Kent Regt. 8 O.R.Wounded 1 O.R.Missing. 18th K.R.R.C. 8 O.R. Wounded.	
27th		A quieter day on the whole. The area round WHITE CHATEAU was shelled. 122nd Infantry Brigade Assembly Instructions issued. 122nd Infantry Brigade R.E.& Pioneer Instructions issued. 122nd Infantry Brigade Machine Gun and Trench Mortar Instructions issued.	App.9 " 10. " 11
		A message was received saying that on the 8th Army Front the enemy had evacuated his Front Line and an idea was abroad that he was retreating. Strong Patrols were ordered to be pushed out, so one went out from the 11th R.W.Kent Regt. to reconnoitre OBLIQUE TRENCH (Ref:- Map 1/10,000 WYTSCHAETE) but were heavily bombed and forced to retire. Another from the 18th Kings Royal Rifle Corps went out from O 11.a 4.4. and went forward for 200 yards and saw none of the enemy. Casualties.- 12th E.Surrey Regt. 2 Officers Wounded 1 O.R.Wounded. 11th R.W.Kent Regt. 19 O.R.Wounded. 122nd Machine Gun Coy. 2 O.R.Wounded.	
28th		A quiet day on the whole. At 1 a.m. the enemy shelled our Left Battalion's front line with 77s but did not do much damage. Message received that a daylight Patrol had gone out from the 18th K.R.R.C. of which a report is attached. Casualties. 15th Hampshire Regt. 5 O.R.Wounded. 11th R.W.Kent Regt. 1 O.R.Wounded. Captain FOX 18th K.R.R.C. missing from Reid referred to in App.12, returns Wounded. The man of the 11th R.W.Kent Regt. reported missing from the Patrol on the night 27/28th, today returned to our lines.	" 12
29th		122nd Infantry Brigade Instructions on (a) Consolidation and Method of holding the line, and Instructions regarding the disposal of Prisoners of War issued. A quiet day in our forward area. OPTIC AVENUE was slightly shelled during the morning. In the back areas things were more lively, SPOIL BANK was intermittently shelled and a 4.5 How battery near it. Casualties 11th R.W.Kent Regt. 3 O.R.Wounded. 18th K.R.R.C. 1 O.R.Killed 3 O.R. Wounded. 122nd M.G.Coy. 2 O.R.Wounded.	" 13 a. & b.

Army Form C. 2118

WAR DIARY
or
INTELLIGENCE SUMMARY
(Erase heading not required.)

Instructions regarding War Diaries and Intelligence Summaries are contained in F. S. Regs., Part II. and the Staff Manual respectively. Title Pages will be prepared in manuscript.

Place	Date	Hour	Summary of Events and Information	Remarks and references to Appendices
JULY 1917			122nd Infantry Brigade.	
	30th 31st		A quiet day on the whole. Units report arrival into their Battle Headquarters at 7 a.m. From midnight onwards the WHITE CHATEAU WOODS were barraged steadily until ZERO Hour (3.50 a.m.) Assembly was satisfactory on the whole. The Left Battalion (11th Royal West Kent Regt) were had their left company observed during Assembly and the enemy put a barrage down some 100 yards behind it. Report on Battle, Messages and Maps, are to be included in the War Diary for the forthcoming month. Casualties for 30th - 12th E.Surrey Regt. 1 O.R.Wounded 15th Hampshire Regt. 2 O.R.Wounded. 11th R.W.Kent Regt. 3 O.R.Wounded. 18th K.R.R.Corps. 1 O.R.Wounded. [signature] Brigadier General. Commanding 122nd Infantry Brigade. August 2nd 1917.	

I.

Verbal Messages night of 5/6th July.

9.20 pm. Stand's report from rear Hqrs.
Enemy massing opposite HOLLEBEKE
from direction of canal.
Guns ordered to fire on S.O.S. lines.
Repeated to division.

9.30. 124 Bde report that their left
Batt'n has sent up S.O.S.
Situation been given.
Guns ordered to slow down.

9.50 F.O.O. reports having seen 2 parties
of the enemy in front of HOLLEBEKE.
S.O.S. goes up again. Rate of
fire increased to 4 per minute.
124 Bde informed.
DINGO data barrage fires.

9.55. O.C. HAMLET to G.O.C. Enemy are
attacking HOLLEBEKE.

10.7. HAMLET reports that at 9.30pm all
our posts were intact — report came
from wounded officer.

10.12. Wounded officer, through artillery
that there is no attack on our right.

10.14. DINGO told to fire bursts in front of
Green line along canal.

II.

10.25. Artillery slowing down in accordance with request of HOOGE. Firing bursts along canal bank.

10.40. Right Bde. (57th) informed of situation as known. Their left Company has no troubles at all — all quiet.

10.50. Hants report:—
Situation Normal. Messenger has come from FORRET for centre post.

10.51. G.O.C. 6/41
Situation at HOLLEBEKE normal. Artillery has been stopped.
Confirming wire sent. Bdes on left and right notified.

11 pm. HOOLET reports
Enemy attacked on left and against HOLLEBEKE & was driven off.
Divn. informed — Confirmed by wire to Bdes on right and left.

11.15. Left 57th Bde report that their post and ours at FORRET Farm were attacked, but attack was completely repulsed & both posts are now intact.

SECRET.

Copy No. 10.

122nd INFANTRY BRIGADE ORDER No.127.

Ref:- Map 28 S.W.2. Edition 5A 1/10,000

1.- An Attack will be carried out by the 41st Division at a date to be fixed later, in conjunction with the 19th Division of the IX Corps on the Right, and the 24th Division of the II Corps on the Left.

2.- The Objectives of the 41st Division are shown on the attached Map 'B'.

   1st Objective. RED LINE, i.e. The enemy's Front Line.

   2nd Objective. BLUE LINE, i.e. FORRET FARM - HOLLEBEKE cross roads and new German Trench.

   3rd Objective. GREEN LINE, i.e. Final Objective.

   Should the opportunity offer, it may be decided to exploit a further advance on ZANVOORDE. One Brigade of the 47th Division will be held in readiness for this.

3.- 122nd Infantry Brigade will attack on that part of Divisional Front which is South of the CANAL.
123rd Infantry Brigade will be on the Left, and a Brigade of the 19th Division on the Right of 122nd Infantry Brigade

   1 Section 228th Field Company R.E. will be attached to 122nd Infantry Brigade for the attack.

4.- The attack will be carried out by 2 Battalions:-
The 18th King's Royal Rifle Corps on the Right, and
The 11th Bn. Royal West Kent Regt. on the Left.

   The Objectives of 122nd Infantry Brigade will be:-

   1st Objective. RED LINE within Brigade Boundary.

   2nd Objective. (BLUE and GREEN) LINES within Brigade Boundary.

   Objectives of Battalions, and Boundary between them, are shown on attached Map 'A', which also shows Brigade Boundaries.

5.- Consolidation will be carried out as under:-
On capture of RED LINE Strong Points will be constructed by:-

   18th Bn. King's Royal Rifle Corps at approx. O 11 b 25.65.
                                                               O 5 d 55.20.

   11th Bn. Royal West Kent Regt.   at approx. O 5 d 6.6.
                                                             O 6 a 05.00.

   On capture of BLUE and GREEN LINES Strong Points will be established by -
   18th Kings Royal Rifle Corps at approx. O 11 b 4.0.
                                            O 12 a 2.2.

   11th Bn. Royal West Kent Regt.   "   O 12 d 5.8.

A Garrison/-

A Garrison of 1 Platoon with Lewis Gun and also a Vickers Gun will be told off in advance to act as garrison of each Strong Point.
The GREEN LINE will eventually form our Front Line, and the Strong Points in the neighbourhood of this Line will serve as basis for its consolidation. The Line will be sighted by the Officers on the spot with due regard to observation over the ground in the immediate front. Posts will be pushed forward as far as the artillery barrage permits, to cover the consolidation of the GREEN LINE. These Posts will be withdrawn under orders of Battalion Commanders, when no longer required.

6.- There will be a preliminary bombardment lasting several days.

7.- Approximate positions of Assembling for Battalions are shown in attached Map 'A'. Units will assemble on Y/Z Night under orders to be issued later, and will be in position by Zero minus one hour.
Positions of Headquarters, Communication Trenches, Tracks, Tramways, Dumps, R.A.Ps are shown in attached Map 'A'.

8.- Formation and Method of Attack.

The leap-frog method will be employed by each of the Assaulting Battalions, who will advance in two waves. Each Battalion will be on a two Company Front, with each Company on a FOUR Platoon Front.

1st Wave. Will capture RED LINE, Mop it up and construct and garrison Strong Points as already detailed. Special parties will be told off by 18th Bn. King's Royal Rifle Corps for mopping up dug-outs in OBLONG ALLEY, HOLLEBEKE ROAD between jumping off place and RED LINE, part of OPTIC SUPPORT included in RED LINE, OBLIQUE ROW - HOLLEBEKE ROAD between jumping off place and RED LINE.

Special Parties will be told off by 11th Bn. Royal West Kent Regt. for mopping up OBLIQUE TRENCH, Dug-outs in Wood at O 5 d 8.4½.

2nd Wave. Will pass through 1st Wave and take BLUE and GREEN LINES,- Mop up area between RED and GREEN LINES - make Strong Points about GREEN LINE already detailed - consolidate about this line - push out Posts to limit of barrage.

18th Bn. King's Royal Rifle Corps will detail special mopping up parties for dug-outs at FERRET FARM, OBLONG ALLEY - HOLLEBEKE Road between RED and GREEN LINES, OBLIQUE ROW - HOLLEBEKE ROAD between RED and GREEN LINES, HOLLEBEKE VILLAGE and DUGOUTS South-East of Village on BLUE LINE.

11th Bn. Royal West Kent Regt. will detail special mopping up parties for OPTIC SUPPORT, VERBRANDEN - HOLLEBEKE Road between RED and GREEN LINES, C.T. between WOOD at O 5 d 8.4½. and GREEN LINE.

9.- Time Table of attack and artillery Barrage will follow. The rate of the Creeping Barrage will be 100 yards in 4 minutes. The Barrage will advance to a final position 400 yards beyond the GREEN LINE.

10. The Attack/-

10.- The Attack will be covered by a Machine Gun Barrage. O.C. 122nd Machine Gun Company will detail one Section to accompany each of the Assaulting Battalions to follow Second Wave. One gun will be told off to Strong Point mentioned in para.5.
Positions will be reconnoitred for one Section of guns to take up positions behind OPTIC TRENCH to cover the front with direct fire in case of counter attack.
Remaining Section will be in Reserve.

11.- O.C. 122nd Trench Mortar Battery will detail one Mortar and Carriers with 40 rounds to accompany each of the Assaulting Battalions.
One Mortar will be attached to 12th East Surrey Regt. and one to 15th Hampshire Regiment for the day of the Attack.

12.- Not more than 500 men will be taken into action by any Battalion on the day of the attack, irrespective of their strength.

13.- Kit and Equipment will be as carried on June 7th 1917.

14.- Further Instructions will be issued on the following:-
1. Artillery Instructions.
2. R.E. and Pioneers.
3. Signal Communications and Instructions for CONTACT AEROPLANES.
4. Machine Gun and Light Trench Mortar arrangements.
5. LIAISON.
6. Administrative Instructions.
7. Assembly.

15.- ACKNOWLEDGE.

16.- NOTE:- No papers dealing with this Scheme are to be kept in the Line forward of Brigade Headquarters.

[signature]
Captain.
Brigade Major.
122nd Infantry Brigade.

Issued at.......
18th July 1917.

```
Copy No. 1 Filed.
     No. 2 War Diary.
     No. 3 41st Division (G).
     No. 4 12th E.Surrey Regt.
     No. 5 15th Hants.Regt.
     No. 6 11th R.W.Kent Regt.
     No. 7 18th K.R.R.C.
     No. 8 122nd M.G.Coy.
     No. 9 122nd T.M.Battery.
     No.10 123rd Inf.Brigade.
     No.11 124th Inf.Brigade.
     No.12 228th Field Coy.
     No.13 No.2 Section Sigs.
     No.14 Staff Captain.
```

SECRET   Copy No. 10

ADMINISTRATIVE ARRANGEMENTS
for
Forthcoming Operations, ref:- 122nd Infantry Brigade
Order No.127 dated 18-7-1917.
----

28 S.W.2.
1/10,000.

1.- RATIONS and WATER.

In order to reduce wheeled traffic on roads and tracks on 'Y' day, barrage rations as under will be dumped near forward limit of horse transport.
One day's complete rations for consumption on 'Z' Day.
Sites selected for these dumps are as follows:-
11th Bn. Royal West Kent Regiment.   )
18th Bn. Kings Royal Rifle Corps.   ) WHITE CHATEAU.
122nd Machine Gun Company.   )
122nd Trench Mortar Battery.   )
12th East Surrey Regiment near Battalion Headquarters at O 4 b 2.3.
15th Bn. Hampshire Regiment near Battalion Headquarters at O 3 b 9½.9.
Battalion strength has been calculated at 600.
Machine Gun Company   -do-   220.
Trench Mortar Battery. -do-   80.
One third gallons of water per man per diem in petrol tins will be dumped with these rations.
The method of drawing these rations and petrol tins will be issued later.
Rations for consumption on 'Z' plus 1 and subsequent days will be delivered as normally by pack or wheeled transport under Battalion arrangements.

2.- WATER.

Details of water supply in Forward Area are as shown in Appendix 'A'.
A reserve of water carts is being placed at the disposal of the Division. In the event of the pipe line being broken, these carts will be put forward to a convenient central point (probably near Bridge I 33 d 3.6.) where water carrying parties can exchange empty for full petrol tins.

3.- S.A.A., GRENADES and LIGHT TRENCH MORTAR AMMUNITION.

Divisional Dump will be at N 4 c 5.2.
Brigade Dump will be at   O 3 b 8.9. or O 4 a 1.7.
Dumps for the two Assaulting Battalions are being established in recesses in OPAL RESERVE.
These are being prepared and partially filled by 47th Division.
Appendix 'B' shows amounts allotted for Operations.

4.- R.E. STORES.

Divisional R.E. Dump will be at BRASSERIE N 6 a 1.1.
An Advanced R.E. Dump is being formed at OAK DUMP O 3 b 9.7.

5.- MEDICAL.

Regimental Aid Posts:-
    18th Bn. King's Royal Rifle Corps - O 3 d 6.8.
    11th Bn. Royal West Kent Regt.   - O 4 a 6.2.
Collecting Post,- SHELLEY LANE I 32 d 3.3.
Advanced Dressing Station - VOORMEZEELE I 31 c 4.6.
Collecting Station for Walking Wounded - BRASSERIE N 6 a 2.2.
Main Dressing Station for seriously wounded LA CLYTTE ROAD
                                                  M 6 a 8.8.
Main Dressing Station for Walking Wounded - LA CLYTTE N 7 c 4.5.

6.- Prisoners/-

- 2 -

6.- PRISONERS OF WAR.

Escorts to Prisoners of War being sent back should not exceed 5% of the number of prisoners.
A Relay Post will be formed at the Headquarters of the Battalion in Reserve (15th Bn. Hampshire Regiment) at O 3 b 9.7½., where escorts will be organised from the Battalion in Reserve, and the original escorts returned to their unit.
The Officer in charge of the Cage will give a receipt to the escort for all prisoners handed over to him, and return escorts to their units.
The position of the Cage will be notified later.

7.- STRAGGLER POSTS.

A line of Divisional Straggler Posts will be established at:- O 2 a 4.6.   (BUS HOUSE).
I 31 d 4.4.
I 33 a 2.3.   (BRIDGE).

11th Bn. Royal West Kent Regt. and 18th Bn. King's Royal Rifle Corps will arrange for Posts, found from Regimental Police on all main communication trenches in their area, to be posted previous to Zero Hour.
12th Bn. East Surrey Regt. will establish a Post at OAK DUMP, to be posted before Zero Hour.
Stragglers arrested by Divisional Posts will be handed over to 1st Line Transport of unit, and sent back at first opportunity.

8.- REINFORCEMENT CAMP.

A Divisional Reinforcement Camp will not be formed.
Details left behind under S.S.135 will remain in their Battalion Transport Camp where any Drafts arriving during the Operations will be sent.
Battalions will place an Officer in charge of all personnel with their Transport and he will render return (Appendix 'C') to 2nd.Lieut.A.V. REINER, 12th Bn. East Surrey Regiment, by 12 noon daily. 2nd.Lieut.REINER will be responsible for co-ordinating this return, and will sent it to reach Divisional Headquarters, 'A' & 'Q' Office by 4 p.m. daily.
No personnel is to be sent up to join their units without orders from Divisional Headquarters. Battalions who desire Officers or men to be sent up should wire Brigade Headquarters.

9.- PACKS AND SURPLUS KIT.

Packs and surplus kit will be stored at RENINGHELST in the barn at G 34 d 65.80., the personnel now there will be maintained, no additional men may be sent by units.
In order to admit of great-coats being rapidly issued should opportunity occur, these will be rolled in bundles reparate from the packs.
Men should be warned to leave no private property in their great-coat pockets.

10.- ACKNOWLEDGE.

[signature]
Captain.
Staff Captain.
122nd Infantry Brigade.

18th July 1917.

Copy No. 1 Filed.
No. 2 War Diary.
No. 3 41st Division 'Q'
No. 4 12th E. Surrey Regt.
No. 5 15th Hants. Regt.
No. 6 11th R.W. Kent Regt.
No. 7 18th K.R.R. Corps.

Copy No. 8 122nd M.G.Coy.
No. 9 122nd T.M. Battery.
No.10 123rd Inf. Brigade.
No.11 124th Inf. Brigade.
No.12 226th Field Coy.R.E.
No.13 122nd Bde. Signals.
No.14 Brigade Major.
No.15 Transport Officer.

APPENDIX 'A'

1. Water Cart refilling point - I 31 d 2.4.
2. Water Tanks and Stand Pipes - N 6 a 10.10.
                                             N 5 a 90.95.
                                             N 5 b 30.80.
                                             I 31 d 20.40.
                                             I 31 d 80.85.
                                             O 1 d 35.75.
                                             O 8 a 65.90.
                                             O 9 a 70.20.
                                             I 33 a 50.10. ∅
                                             I 33 c 80.70. ∅
                                             I 33 c 50.45. ∅
                                             I 33 d 30.50. ∅
                                             O 4 a 75.60. ∅

    Tanks marked ∅ mean supply unreliable.

3. Stand Pipes only -   N 6 a 2.9.
                               N 6 b 4.9.

4. Wells.   I 31 c 40.60.)
                               I 31 c 60.40.)
                               O 2 a 60.70.)Notice Board
                               O 3 c 95.10.)erected show
                               I 33 c 80.85.)ing amount of
                               I 32 d 85.20.)chlorination
                               O 10 b 10.40.)required.
                               O 9 d 35.25.

....

APPENDIX 'B'

	BRIGADE DUMP.	Total of FORWARD DUMPS.
S.A.A.	150,000	100,000
No.5 Mill's Bombs.	3,000	2,000
Rifle Grenades and blanks.	1,000	1,000
Stokes Shells with cartridges.	500	500
Very Lights 1"	500	500
Very Lights 1½"	250	250
Webley Pistol S.A.A.	250	250
'P' Grenades.	250	250
S.O.S.) Flares) Rockets) Coloured Very Lights.) Smoke Candles.)	50% of allotment from Division.	50% of allotment from Division.

This does not include the equipment of Bombers, Grenadiers, or any establishment on wheels.

....

APPENDIX 'C'.

RETURN OF PERSONNEL ....

BATTALION.	Details left behind by Battalions.		Reinforcements who have not been out before.		Reinforcements who have been out before.		Sent up to join units.		REMARKS.
	Offrs.	O.Ranks.	Offrs.	O.Ranks.	Offrs.	O.Ranks.	Offrs.	O.Rks.	

Date............................ O. i/c Personnel........................

SECRET.   Copy No. 10

BRIGADE INSTRUCTIONS No. 4.

Ref:- 122nd Infantry Brigade Order No.127 of 18-7-17.

MACHINE GUNS and LIGHT TRENCH MORTARS.

1.- The attack will be supported by a Machine Gun Barrage.

    1 Machine Gun Company   23rd Division.
    1   -do-   -do-   41st Division. (124th M.G.Coy).
    1   -do-   -do-   47th Division.

Portions of 4th and 12th Motor M.G.Batteries will provide the Barrage.
The Divisional Machine Gun Officer, 41st Division will be in Command of the Barrage.

2.- The three Barrage Companies will be organised in six Machine Gun Batteries each consisting of 8 guns, A, B, C, D, E and F Batteries. The approximate positions of these Batteries are shown on the attached Map.

3.- The Barrage will come down at Zero, 500 yards beyond the first Objective - the RED Line. At Zero plus 10 it will lift on to a line 500 yards beyond the final Objective, where it will remain till Zero plus 70.
After this, the Batteries will be ready to answer any S.O.S. Call.
Arrangements will be made whereby all Barrage Batteries can concentrate on to any particular Map square on the Divisional Front.
Rate of fire Zero to Zero plus 20 - 1 belt per gun per 4 minutes.
Rate of fire Zero plus 20 to Zero plus 70 - 1 belt per gun per 8 minutes.

4.- 122nd Machine Gun Company will support the Attack of 122nd Infantry Brigade.
One Section will accompany each of the Assaulting Battalions, closely following the second wave.
One gun will be previously told off to the following Strong Points, which will be dug by the Infantry:-
   at approximately   O 11 b 25.65.)
                          O 5 d 55.20.) 18th K.R.R.C.
                          O 11 b 4.0.) area.
                          O 12 a 2.2.)

                          O 5 d 6.6.   )
                          O 6 a 05.00.) 11th R.W.Kent Regt.
                          O 12 a 5.8.) area.

Positions will be reconnoitred for one Section of Guns to take up behind OPTIC TRENCH to cover the front with direct fire in case of counter attack.- Remaining Section will be in reserve.

5.- The two Infantry men per gun, who have been attached to 122nd Machine Gun Company, will remain attached throughout the Operations.

6.- With aid of attached Infantry, and YUKON Packs, 3,000 rounds in belts will be carried with each gun.

7.- Position of/-

- 2 -

7.- Position of O.C. 122nd Machine Gun Company will be with Section of Guns in vicinity of OPTIC TRENCH.

8.- O.C. 122nd Light Trench Mortar Battery will detail one mortar and Carriers with 40 rounds to accompany each of the Assaulting Battalions. Battalion Commanders will call upon the Trench Mortars for assistance should the advance be held up by any fortified post.
On capture of final Objective, Officers in Charge Trench Mortar teams will select positions whence to cover consolidation of GREEN LINE.
One Mortar will be attached to 12th East Surrey Regiment, and one to 15th Hampshire Regiment for the day of the Attack.

9.- Position of O.C. 122nd Light Trench Mortar Battery will be at Light Trench Mortar Battery Headquarters in the Line.

10.- ACKNOWLEDGE.

20th July 1917.

Captain.
Brigade Major.
122nd Infantry Brigade.

Copy No. 1 Filed.
No. 2 War Diary.
No. 3 41st Division. (G).
No. 4 12th E.Surrey Regt.
No. 5 15th Hants.Regt.
No. 6 11th R.W.Kent Regt.
No. 7 18th K.R.R.C.
No. 8 122nd M.G.Coy.
No. 9 122nd T.M.Battery.
No.10 123rd Inf.Brigade.
No.11 124th Inf.Brigade.
No.12 56th Inf.Brigade.
No.13 228th Field Coy.R.E.
No.14 No.2 Sect.41st Div.Sigs.
No.15 Staff Captain.

Map not attached

SECRET. *acked* Copy No. 10

BRIGADE INSTRUCTIONS No. 5

Ref:- 122nd Infantry Brigade Order No.127 of 18-7-17.

LIAISON

1.- In order to distribute and to obtain definite information quickly with reference to progress of our own Infantry and R.A., and those of formations and units on either flank, the following arrangements will be made for LIAISON.-

(a) One Officer from Right Double Group Heavy Artillery, and one from the Divisional Artillery, will be attached to Brigade Headquarters.

(b) The 56th Infantry Brigade will be on the Right of the 122nd Infantry Brigade.
2nd.Lieut. TAMBLYN, 12th East Surrey Regiment, will act as LIAISON Officer with this Brigade, and will report with two cyclist orderlies to Headquarters at DOME HOUSE on 'Y' Day at a time to be notified later.

(c) Arrangements will be made for flank Company Commanders of Brigades to meet at an early date.
During the action touch will be maintained between flank companies of Brigades by means of Runners.
The Battalion on the Right of the 18th King's Royal Rifle Corps will be the 7th Bn. North Lancashire Regt., Headquarters in DENYS WOOD., and the Battalion on the Left of the 11th Bn. Royal West Kent Regt. will be the 23rd Middlesex Regiment.

2.- On "Z/A" and subsequent night the normal Liaison between the Divisional Artillery and Battalions (i.e. F.O.O. at Battalion Headquarters) will be maintained.

3.- ACKNOWLEDGE.

Captain.
Brigade Major.
122nd Infantry Brigade.

20th June 1917.

Copy No. 1 Filed.
No. 2 War Diary.
No. 3 41st Division. (G).
No. 4 12th E.Surrey Regt.
No. 5 15th Hants.Regt.
No. 6 11th R.W.Kent Regt.
No. 7 18th K.R.R.C.
No. 8 122nd M.G.Coy.
No. 9 122nd T.M.Battery.
No.10 123rd Inf.Brigade.
No.11 124th Inf.Brigade.
No.12 56th Inf.Brigade.
No.13 228th Field Coy.
No.14 No.2 Sect.41st Div.Sigs.
No.15 Staff Captain.
No.16 C.R.A.

S E C R E T   Ackd   B.M.717/66/-

Copy No. 10

AMENDMENT TO 122nd INFANTRY BRIGADE INSTRUCTION No. 4.

MACHINE GUNS.

Para.3   delete first sub-para, i.e. lines one to four, and substitute:-

"The barrage will come down 400 yards beyond the BLUE LINE and remain till Zero plus 20 minutes.

At Zero plus 20 minutes M.G. barrage lifts to a line 800 yards beyond the GREEN LINE and remains till Zero plus 70 minutes".

ACKNOWLEDGE.

                                           A.Y. Graham Thomson
                                                     Captain.
21-7-17.   Brigade Major.
                                       122nd Infantry Brigade.

To all recipients of 122nd Inf.Bde.Instruction No.4., dated 20th July 1917.

SECRET   Copy No. ....

ADDENDUM
to
122nd Infantry Brigade Order No. 127.

1.- The Time Table of the attack and Creeping Barrage will be as under:-

Zero minus one hour.	Infantry are formed up in Assembly positions.
ZERO HOUR.	Creeping Barrage comes down from 100 to 150 yards in front of OPTIC TRENCH, thence to O 5 d 60.55 to O 5 d 65.75 to O 6 a 2.4.
Zero plus 4 minutes.	Barrage creeps forward.
Zero plus 8 "	Infantry take RED LINE.
Zero plus 18 "	Barrage halts on BLUE LINE.
Zero plus 22 "	Barrage creeps forward again.
Zero plus 26 "	Barrage halts on GREEN LINE.
Zero plus 40 "	Barrage creeps forward again.
Zero plus 44 "	Infantry take GREEN LINE.
Zero plus 56 "	Barrage halts 400 yards beyond GREEN LINE.

2.- Each Battery of the Creeping Barrage will on reaching the GREEN LINE, fire 2 smoke shells, to assist the infantry in locating this line on the ground.

This is, however, only intended as an additional aid, and all officers and N.C.Os should know the time at which the Infantry, closely following the barrage, should be on the GREEN LINE, and should note the time, it is suggested, on the face of a watch.

July 22nd 1917.
                                                        Captain.
                                                     Brigade Major.
                                                 122nd Infantry Brigade.

            Copy No. 1 Filed.
                 No. 2 War Diary.
                 No. 3 41st Division.
                 No. 4 12th E.Surrey Regt.
                 No. 5 15th Hants.Regt.
                 No. 6 11th R.W.Kent Regt.
                 No. 7 18th K.R.R.C.
                 No. 8 122nd M.G.Coy.
                 No. 9 122nd T.M.Battery.
                 No.10 123rd Inf.Bde.
                 No.11 124th Inf.Bde.
                 No.12 56th Inf.Bde.
                 No.13 228th Field Cot.R.E.
                 No.14 Bde.Signal Section.
                 No.15 Staff Captain.

SECRET. Map not attached   Copy No. 10.

Acked

122nd INFANTRY BRIGADE INSTRUCTIONS. No.1.

Ref:- 122nd Infantry Brigade Order No.127 of 18-7-1917.

ARTILLERY INSTRUCTIONS.

1.- The Attack to be made by 122nd Infantry Brigade will be covered by the following Groups of Artillery from Right to Left:-
   - ST. ELOI GROUP.
   - OOSTHOEK GROUP.
   - CHATEAU GROUP.
   - CANAL GROUP.

2.- The roll of the artillery is as follows:-

   (a) **Preliminary Period.**

   Destructive shoots, wire-cutting and harassing fire.

   (b) **Bombardment.**

   Probable duration 5 to 7 days, during which enemy works, strong points, Headquarters, telephone exchanges, etc., will be demolished. Wire-cutting will continue, and enemy approaches will be kept under fire both by day and night.

   (c) **Barrage.**

   The barrage in support of the attack will consist of a creeping barrage of 18-prs. firing shrapnel only, preceding the Infantry in lifts of 100 yards every 4 minutes, and a standing barrage of 18-prs. and 4.5" Hows., on certain definite points and trenches, and a Heavy Artillery barrage on trench systems, etc. The barrage will be of a strength of approximately 1 18-pr. to 15 yards of front.

   (d) **Protective Barrage.**

   Consolidation during its earlier stages will be covered by a protective barrage on a line about 400 yards beyond GREEN LINE.
   This barrage will consist of 18-prs. firing shrapnel and H.E., 75% of this protective barrage, will at intervals search and sweep forward 500 yards beyond the line of the protective barrage.

   (e) **Fleeting opportunities.**

   (a) From Zero till creeping barrage reaches final barrage line, 3 18-pr. Batteries and 1 4.5" How. Battery will be available to deal with fleeting opportunities.

   (b) After creeping barrage reaches final barrage line, one half of the total Field Artillery covering the Division will be available to deal with fleeting opportunities in their respective Group zones.

   (f) Vigorous counter battery work.

para.3/-

3.- Map showing Creeping Barrage and Zones covered by different
     Groups attached.

4.- ACKNOWLEDGE.

[signature]

Captain.
Brigade Major.
22nd July 1917.   122nd Infantry Brigade.

Copy No. 1 Filed.
     No. 2 War Diary.
     No. 3 41st Division (G).
     No. 4 12th E.Surrey Regt.
     No. 5 15th Hants.Regt.
     No. 6 11th R.W.Kent Regt.
     No. 7 18th K.R.R.C.
     No. 8 122nd M.G.Coy.
     No. 9 122nd T.M.Battery.
     No.10 123rd Inf.Bde.
     No.11 124th Inf.Bde.
     No.12 228th Field Coy.R.E.
     No.13 Bde.Signal Section.
     No.14 Staff Captain.

SECRET.   *Ackd*   Copy No. 10.

BRIGADE INSTRUCTIONS No. 3.

Ref:- 122nd Infantry Brigade Order No.127 of 18-7-17.

SIGNAL COMMUNICATION.

1.- System of Communication from Brigade to Battalion Headquarters will be as follows:-

   (a) The main channel of communication from Brigade to Battalion Headquarters of Assaulting Battalions will be by buried cable.

   (b) Runner Routes will be established and flagged from Brigade to Battalion Headquarters, under Brigade arrangements; a runner Relay Post manned by the Brigade, being established at Support Battalion (12th East Surrey Regt.) Headquarters, under charge of Lieut. WALKER, 12th East Surrey Regiment.

   (c) A Wireless set is being set up at O 4 b 60.50, sending to a parent station at F C 2.
   There will be two Brigade Runners at O 4 b 60.50 to take messages forward to Battalion Headquarters. Battalions will have runners available to take messages to this wireless station for transmission to Brigade.

2.- Forward of Battalion Headquarters, battalions will be responsible for maintaining communications.
Runners' routes will be established and flagged, and relay posts established between Battalion Headquarters and Company Headquarters, and lateral routes between units.
The responsibility for all lateral communication is from Right to Left.

3.- In addition to the above means of communication a system of Power Buzzers and Amplifiers will be maintained by personnel of Brigade Signal Section.
The system is shewn on attached plan.
Amplifiers and Power Buzzers will be situated, and work as under:-

   1 Amplifier and Power Buzzer   at Support Battalion (12th East Surrey Regt.) Headquarters, working to Amplifier and Power Buzzer at Headquarters of Assaulting Battalions.

   1 Amplifier and two Power Buzzers will be placed in the OPAL RESERVE before the attack commences, and be ready to move forward as soon as the assaulting troops advance. These parties will be under the charge of Lieut. TAYLOR, Essex Regt., attached 18th K.R.R.Corps.

   The Amplifier and one Power Buzzer will be placed in position in our old Front Line near junction of OAK AVENUE and OPTIC TRENCH.
   The remaining Power Buzzer will be carried forward behind the second wave along OAK AVENUE - HOLLEBEKE Road.
   It will be established at a point near O 11 b 80.70.
   The position of this Power Buzzer will be marked by a Blue and white flag. Battalion Signalling Officers concerned will arrange runners to this Station, which will work to AMPLIFIER and POWER BUZZER in OPTIC TRENCH, these latter instruments will be in communication with Battalion Headquarters concerned.

4.- Four pigeons.

4.- Four pigeons will be allotted to each Battalion in the line every day. Battalion pigeoneers will report at Brigade Headquarters to draw birds each morning at 10 a.m.
Pigeon refilling point is at I 31 c 8.6.
In special cases birds can be drawn at any hour.

5.- During Offensive Operations, Code calls will be used in conjunction with single letters representing sentences, as shewn in the attached list, for all forms of signalling:-
The message will, for example take the following form -

"CD NNN CDY 10.20 a.m." meaning "To 122nd Infantry Brigade, We are short of ammunition, from 11th Bn. Royal West Kent Regt., 10.20 a.m.".
Responsibility for coding and decoding is on sender and receiver of messages and not on the signallers.

6.- One Contact Aeroplane will be up from Zero (if light enough) till 3 hours after Zero.
Aeroplanes of the Xth Corps Squadron are distinguished by three broad white bands on the fuselage, and contact aeroplanes are further distinguished by the attachment of a black board on the left lower plane.
These machines will be furnished with wireless but will only use it for the purpose of reporting a counter-attack or transmitting an Infantry message calling for barrage.
Contact aeroplanes will call for flares by firing a white light, and sounding a Klaxon Horn.
Leading Infantry will light flares approximately at the following time:-

Zero plus 60 minutes   (GREEN LINE).

Infantry must, however, ensure that the aeroplane is calling for flares before lighting up.
Patrols temporarily pushed forward to cover consolidation will not light flares.

7.- A wireless aeroplane will be up throughout the day from one hour after Zero for the purpose of looking out for counter-attacks. In event of a counter-attack developing this machine will call on the Artillery by the Zone Call and will warn the Infantry by Flares; a green flare will signify that the attack is North of the Canal, and a red flare South of the Canal.
The Zone Call will give the position and direction of movement of the enemy's infantry, and this information will be immediately communicated by the Artillery to the Infantry Brigadier concerned.
This machine will also transmit Infantry messages calling for barrage.
As a further measure against counter-attacks, should any of the aeroplanes working with Infantry or Artillery see parties of hostile infantry quitting their trenches and advancing in the open in the direction of our lines, the Observer will send down by wireless "S.O.S." followed by Zone Call - no map co-ordinates will be given. This will constitute a request to our artillery to put up a barrage on their S.O.S. lines in that particular zone.
This machine will keep under careful observation the enemy's position at ZANDVOORDE with a view to notifying at once any signs of retirement by the enemy who may possibly be affected by a success by our troops in the direction of TOWER HAMLETS.

8.- The lighting/-

- 3 -

8.- The lighting of flares should be supplemented by WATSON'S Fans, or by waving of helmets, handkerchiefs, maps, papers, mess tins or any light coloured objects.

9.- Brigade and Battalion Headquarters will have their ground signal sheets and call letters sewn on canvas. These should be kept rolled up and only exposed, when the Contact Aeroplane calls.

10.- ACKNOWLEDGE.

[signature]

Captain.
Brigade Major.
122nd Infantry Brigade.

July 22nd 1917.

Copy No. 1 Filed.
No. 2 War Diary.
No. 3 41st Division. (G).
No. 4 12th E.Surrey Regt.
No. 5 15th Hants.Regt.
No. 6 11th R.W.Kent Regt.
No. 7 18th K.R.R.C.
No. 8 122nd M.G.Coy.
No. 9 122nd T.M.Battery.
No.10 123rd Inf.Bde.
No.11 124th Inf.Bde.
No.12 228th Field Coy.R.E.
No.13 56th Inf.Bde.
No.14 Bde.Signal Section.
No.15 Staff Captain.

CODE OF SIGNALS FOR OFFENSIVE OPERATIONS ONLY.

By Signal.	Meaning.
A	No signs of enemy ahead.
B	Enemy are retiring at..........
C	Held up by barrage at..........
D	Held up by Strong Point at........
F	Enemy offering strong resistance at........
G	Further bombardment required.
H	Lengthen range.
I	Am in touch with Battalion on my Right.
J	Raise barrage.
K	Lower Barrage.
L	Have passed...........(Map square).
M	Enemy apparently preparing to attack.
N	Short of ammunition.
O	Barrage wanted at........
P	Reinforcements wanted at........
Q	Am in touch with Battalion on my left.
R	Am still advancing.
S	Artillery target at........
T	Tank disabled at...........
U	Tanks have reached........
V	Tanks required at..........
W	Short of water..
X	Held up by machine gun fire.........
Y	Short of grenades.
Z	Held up by wire at........
O.K.	We are all right.

The map location of the point of the line to which reference is made will be given, if necessary, by the clock code, the position of the sender being considered as the centre of the clock face and the hour 12 being always taken as pointing due North. The distance in yards from the point it is desired to describe will be given by a letter of the alphabet, A representing 50 yds; B 100 yds; C 200; D 300; and so on. The direction will be given by the hour on the imaginary clock face, e.g. if it were necessary to ask for the range to be lengthened at a point 400 yds N.W. of Bn.H.Q. the message would be H H H E 10; H H H being acknowledged by T and the whole message by the code letters of the sender followed by R.D. Distances of 150, 250 yds &c. will be given by a two letter signal, e.g. B A = 150, C A = 250.

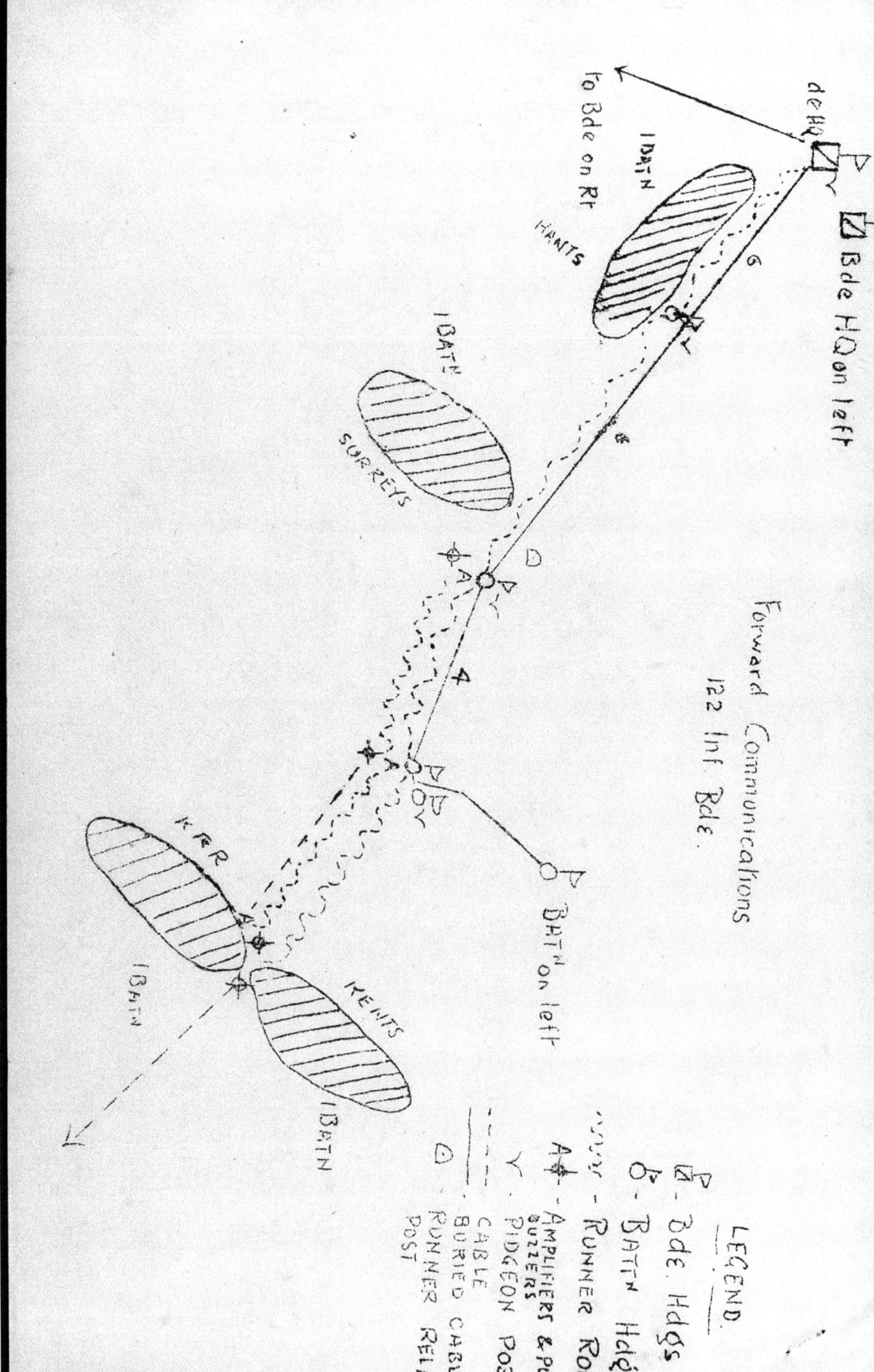

SECRET   Copy No. 10

BRIGADE INSTRUCTIONS NO. 8.

Ref:- 122nd Infantry Brigade Order No.127 of 18-7-17.

ARRANGEMENTS FOR DISPOSAL OF PRISONERS OF WAR, & CAPTURED DOCUMENTS

1.- The Corps Cage, which will also be used as the Divisional Cage, is situated at 28 N 3 a Central.

2.- All prisoners will be taken to the BRASSERIE 28 N 6 a 10.10., where they will be handed over to the A.P.M.

3.- No prisoners will be marched forward of CORPS CAGE.

4.- A special Section has been detailed to collect documents etc., from the battlefield.
This Section will wear brassards marked 'INTELLIGENCE'.

5.- All documents, etc., found on the battlefield will be forwarded to Brigade Headquarters for transmission to the Corps Cage.

6.- Identity discs are **not** to be removed from German dead unless especially asked for.

7.- In order to obtain the Order of Battle it is necessary to know where prisoners were captured. Prisoners are, as a rule, unable to give this information. Escorts on taking over prisoners in the trenches should ascertain where or by whom they were captured and report this information to the representative of the A.P.M. at the BRASSERIE.

8.- Escorts will ensure:-
(a) that Officers, N.C.Os and men are always kept apart and not allowed to converse with each other.
(b) that no documents are destroyed by prisoners on their way to the Cage.

9.- ACKNOWLEDGE.

July 22nd 1917.
             Captain.
            Brigade Major.
           122nd Infantry Brigade.

Copy No. 1 Filed.
No. 2 War Diary.
No. 3 41st Division.(G).
No. 4 12th E.Surrey Regt.
No. 5 15th Hants.Regt.
No. 6 11th R.W.Kent Regt.
No. 7 18th K.R.R.C.
No. 8 122nd M.G.Coy.
No. 9 122nd .M.Battery.
No.10 123rd Inf.Bde.
No.11 124th Inf.Bde.
No.12 228th Field Coy.R.E.
No.13 Bde.Signal Section.
No.14 Staff Captain.

SECRET.   Copy No. 10.

BRIGADE INSTRUCTIONS No. 2

Ref:- 122nd Infantry Brigade Order No.127 of 18-7-17.

R.E. & PIONEERS.

1.- R.E. and Pioneers will be employed on the following work in 122nd Infantry Brigade Area on 'Z' Day and 'Z/A' Night.

	Sect.No.	
1st Canadian T.C. H.Q.SPOIL BANK.	1	Reconnoitre and search for/deep dugouts and mine charges in or about HOLLEBEKE Village.
228th Field Coy.R.E.	1	Under 2/Lt.ADAIR R.E. with attached platoon of 18th K.R.R.C. under 2/Lt. LANGSTON 18th K.R.R.C. will be attached to 122nd Inf. Brigade for the attack. They will assemble in OLD GERMAN Front Line on 'Y/Z' Night under orders to be issued later, and be prepared to move up and commence to open up German C.T. from OBLIQUE TRENCH O 5 d 60.65 to BLUE LINE, or if this appears impracticable to commence a new C.T. forward from OBLIQUE TRENCH.
ø when ordered by G.O.C.122nd Inf.Bde.		
-do-	2) 3) 4)	Consolidate and wire position on RED LINE and old front line South of CANAL.
237th Field Coy.R.E.		Construction of pontoon bridge across CANAL at O 4 a 7.7.
19th Bn.Middlesex Regt. (Pioneers).	B Coy.	Continue OPTIC AVENUE to the BLUE LINE at about O 11 b 7 3, and maintain OPTIC RD and Track from ST.ELOI to OPTIC AVENUE.
-do-	E Coy.	Maintain tramline system from SHELLEY DUMP and from Brickstack to R.A.P's No.3 and 4 at O 4 a 6.2. and O 3 d 8.6. respectively.

2.- R.E.DUMPS will be established as under:-
   Main Divisional Dump.   BRASSERIE   N 6 a 1.1.
   Advanced Divisional Dump. VOORMEZEELE I 31 a 4.1.
   Right Sector Forward Dump. OAK DUMP   O 3 b 9.6.
   Right Sector Advanced)   OAK AVENUE   O 5 d 8.3.
   Consolidation Stores.)

3.- ACKNOWLEDGE.

                                                Captain.
                                          Brigade Major.
                                    122nd Infantry Brigade.

24th July 1917.

Copies to All recipients of O.O.127.

SECRET. Copy No...10

AMENDMENT TO BRIGADE INSTRUCTIONS NO.2.

Ref:- 122nd Infantry Brigade Order No.127 dated 18-7-1917.

R.E. & PIONEERS.

Reference Brigade Instructions No.2 para.2.
The Map reference of OAK AVENUE DUMP should read O 5 c 8.3.
not O 5 d 8.3. as stated therein.

27-7-17.

Captain.
Brigade Major.
122nd Infantry Brigade.

Copies to all recipients of Brigade Instructions No.2.

Ackd

SECRET   Copy No. 10

BRIGADE INSTRUCTIONS No. 7.

Ref:- 122nd Infantry Brigade Order No.127 dated 18-7-17.

ASSEMBLY.

1.- Units will assemble on 'Y/Z' Night in accordance with the attached Table.
   All Units will be in their Assembly Areas, and Assaulting Troops formed up for the attack at Zero minus 1 hour.

2.- Headquarters of units for the Operations will be established as under by 12 noon on 'Y' Day.

   11th Royal West Kent Regt.   )   O 5 c 5.9.
   18th Kings Royal Rifle Corps.)

   12th East Surrey Regiment.   O 4 b 1.4.

   15th Hampshire Regiment.   O 1 c 9.6.

   122nd Machine Gun Company.   O 4 c 2.3.

   122nd Trench Mortar Battery.   O 1 c 9.6.

3.- Battalion Headquarters will be marked by CODE NAMES painted in large letters on canvas screens as already detailed.

4.- O.C. 122nd Machine Gun Company will arrange direct with O.C. 11th Royal West Kent Regt. and 18th Kings Royal Rifle Corps, rendezvous and position of Assembly of Gun teams going forward.

5.- O.C. 122nd Trench Mortar Battery will detail 1 team with Mortar to report to 11th Royal West Kent Regt., and 2 teams with Mortars to 18th Kings Royal Rifle Corps at 6 p.m. 'Y' Day.

6.- Completion of Assembly will be reported to Brigade Headquarters by code.

7.- 12th East Surrey Regiment will move up three companies to OPAL RESERVE, New Support Trench, and OBLIQUE ROW when attacking Troops move forward.

8.- Reinforcements, aprox. number as under, organised into Companies, platoons, etc., will assemble in BOIS CONFLUENT on 'Y/Z' Night.

   15th Hampshire Regiment.   100.
   11th Royal West Kent Regt.   150.
   18th Kings Royal Rifle Corps.   50.

   Major G.D.AMERY 15th Hampshire Regt. will arrange with O.C. 15th Hampshire Regt. as to accommodation and guides. He will also see the complete party marched off under the Senior Officer with the Details.
   March from WOOD CAMP will be under cover of darkness.
   Head of the Column will pass HALLEBAST CORNER at 10.20 p.m. (column must be clear of HALLEBAST CORNER by 11 p.m.), and proceed via RIDGE WOOD.

9.- ACKNOWLEDGE.

                                              Captain.
                                           Brigade Major.
27th July 1917.   122nd Infantry Brigade.

Copies to all recipients of Brigade Order No.127.

TABLE TO ACCOMPANY BRIGADE INSTRUCTIONS No. 7.

UNIT.	FROM	TO	REMARKS.
10th Kings Royal Rifle Corps.	Present Position.	East of a line drawn North and South through WHITE CHATEAU.	To be East of this line by 11.30 p.m.
11th Royal West Kent Regt.	-do-	-do-	-do-
12th East Surrey Regiment.	-do-	Area about OLD GERMAN Front Line and OAK RESERVE.	Head to cross OLD BRITISH Front Line at 11 p.m. (Coy. from LOCK HOUSE BANK TUNNELS to load).
15th Hampshire Regiment.	-do-	1 Company to LOCK HOUSE BANK TUNNELS I 33 d 1.6.	To arrive 11 p.m.
1 Section 228th Field Coy. R.E. and attached platoon.	-do-	LOCK HOUSE BANK TUNNELS.	To arrive after 11.30 p.m.

SECRET   Copy No. 10

BRIGADE INSTRUCTIONS No. 9.

Ref:- 122nd Infantry Brigade Order No.127 of 18-7-17.

CONSOLIDATION and METHOD of HOLDING NEW LINE.

1.- Consolidation will be proceeded with at once, when the ground is gained. The actual siting of the Strong Points will be decided by the Officers on the spot, who must site their defence works with reference to consolidation parties on either flank, so that these points can be connected up.
Wire and posts will be got up as soon as possible.

2.- Battalions will report early the final Line on which they are consolidating, so that the artillery may be informed.

3.- If O.C. 11th Royal West Kent Regt. or O.C. 18th Kings Royal Rifle Corps require extra parties for carrying forward material, they will notify Brigade Headquarters, stating what they wish carried up, and where it is required

4.- O.C. 11th Royal West Kent Regt. will detail an Officer to reconnoitre suitable places for crossing the CANAL between the bend and the GREEN LINE.
The C.R.E. is arranging to throw footbridges across at points selected.

5.- On 'A' day or 'A/B' Night the 11th Bn. Royal West Kent Regiment will, on receipt of orders from the Brigade, take over a portion of the front North of the CANAL up to the strip of WOOD in O 6 d 2.8½. inclusive, making an additional 250 yards of front.

6.- The 122nd Infantry Brigade Front will be held by two Battalions; the boundary between them will be as already detailed for the Assaulting Battalions in the Attack.
Front Line Battalions will be disposed in depth back to and including OPTIC TRENCH and OBLIQUE TRENCH.
Support Battalion between OPTIC and OBLIQUE TRENCHES and OAK RESERVE, the latter inclusive.
Reserve Battalion. Headquarters and 3 Companies BOIS CONFLUENT, 1 Company in LOCK HOUSE BANK TUNNELS.
Brigade Boundaries will be as at present time, until extra front is taken over by Left Battalion, when new Northern Boundary will be notified.

7.- The main line of Resistance will be OPTIC TRENCH and the line of Strong Points to be constructed on the RED LINE.

8.- 122nd Machine Gun Company will be organised in depth for the defence of the new front.
2 Sections covering GREEN LINE from positions about the RED LINE.
1 Section occupying Supporting Positions about our old Front Line and OBLIQUE TRENCH.
1 Section in RESERVE, in positions selected to cover the Brigade Front by barrage fire.

122nd Trench Mortar Battery will have two mortars covering the GREEN LINE, and one in position in present New Support Line, covering the RED LINE.

9.- C.Ts/-

- 2 -

9.- Communication Trenches will be pushed forward to the GREEN LINE as follows:-

SOUTH of CANAL.

OPTIC AVENUE by 19th Middlesex Regt. (Pioneers).
OAK AVENUE and OBLIQUE ROW by troops of 122nd Infantry Brigade under supervision of C.R.E.

NORTH of CANAL.

OAF AVENUE by 19th Middlesex Regt. (Pioneers).

10.- Units will report Forecast of dispositions at 6 a.m. 'B' Day, to this office by 6 p.m. on 'A' Day.

11.- ACKNOWLEDGE.

29th July 1917.

A Y Graham Thomm
Captain.
Brigade Major.
122nd Infantry Brigade.

Copy No. 1 Filed.
No. 2 War Diary.
No. 3 41st Division (G).
No. 4 12th E.Surrey Regt.
No. 5 15th Hants.Regt.
No. 6 11th R.W.Kent Regt.
No. 7 18th K.R.R.Corps.
No. 8 122nd Machine Gun Coy.
No. 9 122nd Trench Mortar Battery.
No.10 123rd Inf.Brigade.
No.11 124th Inf.Brigade.
No.12 56th Inf.Brigade.
No.13 41st Inf.Brigade.
No.14 228th Field Coy.R.E.
No.15 No.2 Coy.41st Div.Sigs.
No.16 Staff Captain.

CONFIDENTIAL.   No. 5

122nd INFANTRY BRIGADE INTELLIGENCE SUMMARY

6 a.m. to 6 p.m. 28th July 1917.

1.- OPERATIONS.

The usual amount of artillery activity on both sides to-day.
OPAL RESERVE and the Supports of our Right Battalion were
shelled intermittently throughout the morning with 77 mm.
Our left was quieter.
The area round WHITE CHATEAU was shot at and the Northern bank
of the CANAL, 5.9 being used.

2.- ENEMY'S FRONT AND SUPPORT LINES.

Machine Guns.

The Machine Guns which was active against our patrol on the
night 26th/27th, did not fire last night so could not be
definitely located.

The suspected sentry post at the corner of WOOD (O 5 d 7.4.)
was not seen to-day.

3.- LOCATION OF ENEMY.

A strong patrol of the 11th Royal West Kent Regt. attempted to
reconnoitre OBLIQUE TRENCH, but was heavily bombed and
compelled to retire with casualties.

A Patrol of the 18th Kings Royal Rifle Corps went out from
O 11 a 4.4. forward for about 200 yards and found no sign
of enemy occupation.

4.- ENEMY MOVEMENT.

Nil.

5.- GENERAL.

A good deal of aerial activity on both sides.
At 10.15 and 10.35 p.m. last night white lights were dropped
from hostile machines, but no action followed.

LIGHTS.

During a retaliation Barrage, which the enemy put up N. of the
CANAL to-day, double green lights were put up which on four
occasions lengthened the range.

                                            Lieut.
                                    Intelligence Officer.
                              for G.O.C. 122nd Infantry Brigade.

www.ingramcontent.com/pod-product-compliance
Lightning Source LLC
Chambersburg PA
CBHW081534160426
43191CB00011B/1756